DATE DUE

DEMCO NO. 38 - 2980

PETTICOAT SPIES
Six Women Spies
of the Civil War

PETTICOAT SPIES
Six Women Spies of the Civil War

Peggy Caravantes

620 South Elm Street, Suite 223
Greensboro, North Carolina 27406
http://www.morganreynolds.com

PETTICOAT SPIES: SIX WOMEN SPIES OF THE CIVIL WAR

Dedicated to
the memory of
my beloved husband, Ted

Contents

Introduction

The Civil War

When the Confederate troops around Charleston, South Carolina, fired on Fort Sumter on the night of April 12, 1861, the country plunged into the most devastating war in American history.

The roots of the war stretched back to the beginning of the colonial era, when African slaves were brought to America and forced to clear land, work farms and plantations, and run the households of the settlers. While slavery gradually ceased in most of the North, it became an intricate part of the economy in the agrarian South.

Slavery had always been controversial. Several of the nation's founders, such as Alexander Hamilton, John Adams, and John Lauren of South Carolina, advocated ending slavery, while other leaders were slaveholders. Some leaders, such as Thomas Jefferson and George Washington, stated that slavery was an evil and barbaric institution that they wished had never been established in America, yet they themselves owned slaves. Many hoped that slavery would become impractical as the South developed economically.

After Eli Whitney invented the cotton gin at the end of the eighteenth century, the production of cotton in the South became a highly profitable, although labor intensive, industry. As slave labor became more critical to maintaining the lifestyle and well-being of the Southern elite, it became clear to antislavery reformers, called abolitionists, that slavery was not going to wither away. They became convinced that it could only be removed by force. Some abolitionists even argued that the non-slave states should secede from the Union, so as to not be joined with a "slaveocracy."

The abolitionists were frustrated in their efforts to move antislavery into the forefront of American politics, however, until 1846, when it became necessary to decide the future of the vast western territories that had been gained in the Mexican War. Intense debate erupted in Congress and spread throughout the country. Should the new territories, which would eventually become states, be slave or "free-soil"?

Southern leaders argued that if slavery was not allowed in the new territories, it was only a matter of time until they would be so out-numbered that slavery would be made illegal everywhere, either by constitutional amendment or by laws passed in Washington. From their point of view, this was intolerable. They would rather leave the Union and form their own country than allow this to happen.

In addition to the abolitionists in the North, there emerged a group of moderate politicians who argued that although slavery was protected by the Constitution in states where it then existed, slavery could not be allowed to spread into the new territories. In 1856, the Republican Party was created to advocate this opinion. Over the next four years, Abraham Lincoln, an Illinois lawyer and one-time congressman, emerged as one of the most eloquent leaders of the new party. He was nominated to be the Republican candidate for president in 1860.

In the South, leaders such as Senator Jefferson Davis of Mississippi, viewed Lincoln's nomination as a serious threat. Although Lincoln said repeatedly that slavery was constitutionally protected in the states where it had existed before 1846, Southern leaders vowed to remove their states from the Union if he was elected.

After Lincoln's election in November 1860, the states of the lower South began to hold conventions and voted to secede. South Carolina moved first, and it was soon followed by Mississippi, Georgia, and other states. After the firing on Fort Sumter, Virginia and other states of the upper South seceded and the Civil War had begun.

The beginning of the war created a groundswell of support in both the North and the South. Many men signed up to serve in what both sides were convinced would be a short war. Women were routinely barred from military service on both sides. The "weaker" sex was considered unfit for the rigors of military service.

There was one area of warfare, however, where women

were as equally capable as men, if not more so. Who better to nose out secrets from officers of the opposing side than women? Who would suspect that the flirtatious daughter of the plantation owner was actually a wily spy, or that the spinster tending to the prisoners in a filthy Richmond jail was gathering secrets for the hated Yankee army?

This book retells the stories of six women Civil War spies. Although each story is different, these women had three things in common: courage, fierce devotion to her cause, and the will to participate in a war.

Sarah Emma Edmonds
(Library of Congress)

Chapter One

Sarah Emma Edmonds

When Elizabeth Leeper Edmondson gave birth to her fifth daughter, Sarah Emma Evelyn, in December 1841, she sobbed because she had wanted another son to work on the family farm in New Brunswick, Canada. Because her only son had epilepsy, the girls had to help their father, Isaac Edmondson, with the tasks usually done by boys. Emma spent her childhood dressing like a boy and performing farm chores. She developed a strong, lean body that in later years helped her disguise herself as a man named Franklin Thompson.

The family lived comfortably, but Mr. Edmondson's verbal abuse of his wife and his children kept the household tense. He resented having to depend on so many girls for the farm work and considered his son's epilepsy a disgrace. Emma determined never to marry because she did not want any man treating her the way her father treated her mother.

Then when she was only fifteen, a farmer more than

twice her age approached Mr. Edmondson about marrying Emma. Her father not only approved of the marriage but insisted on it. For possibly the only time in her life, Emma's mother decided to defy her husband. Mr. Edmondson ordered his wife to prepare for the wedding. Instead she made secret arrangements for her youngest daughter to leave home. She contacted an old friend who was visiting nearby. Mrs. Edmondson convinced the friend to take Emma with her when she left. A few nights later, Emma crept out of the house. As the stagecoach pulled away, she left behind all ties to her family, including the family name. From then on she used "Edmonds" as her last name.

Miss Annie Moffitt, the lady who helped her escape, owned a hat shop, where Emma worked for the next two years. Emma eventually received word that her father had found her hiding place. As she knew he would force her to marry the older farmer, she disappeared again. She reached another town and decided to disguise herself by cutting her hair short and putting on men's clothing. Emma Edmonds became Franklin Thompson. She had no trouble with her disguise because of her height, dark skin, large features, deep voice, and her strong, flat-chested body.

She soon obtained a job as a Bible salesman, which she held for several years. Then one day she lost all of her money and all but one of her Bibles. She sold the Bible for five dollars and used the money to go to the United States. She was nineteen years old. Emma could not take a boat as most travelers would because she had so little money. Instead she hiked and hitched rides on passing sleighs. In later years she described this trip as the hardest experience of her life.

In 1860, she arrived in Hartford, Connecticut, the location of the Bible publishing house she had worked for. She had frostbitten feet, ragged clothes, and worn boots that barely stayed on her feet. She did not know a single person and had no money. She pawned her watch and a chain to pay room and board at a cheap hotel. She used what little money she had left to buy some men's clothing. The next day Emma went to the publishing house, where she introduced herself as Franklin Thompson. Because of her success as a Bible salesman in Canada, the publisher hired her and provided her with books to sell and money for living expenses. But Emma soon tired of the life of a salesman. By the fall of 1860, she began to search for a new challenge. She decided to follow the advice of the saying, "Go West, Young Man," and got as far as Flint, Michigan.

When the Civil War began in 1861, Emma wanted to show her appreciation to her adopted country. She became a Federal field nurse but decided she could better serve the sick and wounded men if she continued her disguise as Frank Thompson. At that time the army had few specific enlistment standards. Although they required no physical examination, Emma was rejected the first time she applied. At five feet six inches tall, her height did not meet the minimum standard of at least five feet eight inches.

The next spring, Captain William Morse wanted to

get Company F of the Michigan Union Grays to full size. Many of his original volunteers had dropped out because the government had changed the enlistment period from three months to three years. On May 25, 1861, Emma, still disguised as Frank, again went to enlist. The army seemed to be taking anyone who "could carry a musket a few yards without falling down." Emma was accepted as a three-year recruit. Although other soldiers teased her about her little boots, no one saw through her disguise.

As Frank, Emma continued nursing in various camp hospitals. She displayed a gift for nursing and a special ability to calm delirious patients. Not until the Battle of Bull Run did Emma get any battle experience. As she later described it, ". . . the battle began to rage with terrible fury. Nothing could be heard save the thunder of artillery, the clash of steel, and the continuous roar of musketry." Throughout this fierce fighting, she continued to take care of the wounded and dying. She even promised to get last messages and personal items from the dying men to their wives, mothers, and sweethearts. Emma later received this note from the mother of one of these young men: "Oh, how I want to kiss those hands that closed my darling's eye, and those lips which spoke words of comfort to him in a dying hour."

Emma saw stacks of torn, bleeding bodies and heaps of crushed and broken legs and arms. She worked hard to care for those who still had a chance. She knew little of the battle's true progress. At first she did not realize that the Yankee soldiers had started to retreat toward

Sarah Emma Edmonds as Frank Thompson
(Library of Congress)

Washington. When she saw that she was now in enemy territory, she had to escape on foot. She hid in some brush, with the darkness and pouring rains further helping her to escape from the rebels. That night she reached Centreville, Virginia, and from there hurried toward Washington, where she arrived at noon the next day—shoeless and exhausted.

Later that year Colonel Orlando M. Poe appointed Emma, or Frank Thompson, to be the regiment's mail carrier. This job gave Emma many chances to go behind enemy lines to get important information for the Union generals. She went in and out of each camp as quickly as she delivered the mail. No one had the time to study her enough to see through her disguise. As she traveled from one camp to another, she often slept on the ground by a road or in the woods. She did not want to risk discovery of her true identity by sleeping in a camp.

One day Emma had just returned to camp after hunting for fresh food for the patients. She saw some soldiers coming back from a burial and learned they had just buried one of her close friends whom she had known since her childhood in Canada. He had died instantly when a bullet passed through his temple as he rode a picket line. This young man may have been the only person to share her secret that she was a woman in a man's clothes. About midnight that night, Emma knelt beside the grave of her friend and vowed to get revenge for his death.

Word came in 1862 that someone needed to take on the duties of a Federal spy who had just been executed.

Emma saw this as an excellent opportunity to avenge her friend's murder. She spoke to a chaplain who agreed to recommend Frank as a spy. Although spying did not require any special training at that time, three generals questioned her about her view of the rebellion. They asked her why she wanted to become involved in such dangerous work. The generals decided that Frank had the intelligence and physical strength to become a spy, but Emma still had to prove her marksmanship and moral character. Once accepted as a spy, she had only three days to prepare for her first assignment.

Emma had to create her own spy disguises. She disguised her gender and her race for her first spying mission. She bought clothes similar to those worn by plantation slaves. These included woolen pants dyed with willow bark and heavy shoes that were so stiff that several layers of grease were necessary to get them to bend even a little. She had a barber shave her head and then used a silver-nitrate solution to color her head, face, neck, and hands black. She next needed a wig that looked like the woolly hair of a typical slave. She could not find one in Fortress Monroe and had to order a wig from Washington. When it arrived by boat a few days later, Emma completed the disguise of "Ned," as she now called herself. She decided to try out the disguise on a close friend, the chaplain's wife, who did not recognize her at all.

Her first task was to get through the lines at Yorktown and to determine the layout of their defenses. Emma took with her only a few hard crackers and a revolver.

She managed to get past the pickets and behind the rebel lines with no trouble, but she waited until midnight to rest. She had no blanket to put on the cold, damp ground and lay scared and trembling the rest of the night.

The next morning she met a group of slaves as they carried breakfast to Confederate pickets. The slaves shared coffee and cornbread with Emma, and when they returned, she joined them without causing any suspicion. Since the other slaves all had jobs to do, Ned's lack of work soon caught the attention of a rebel officer. He said that everyone at his site had to work and turned Emma over to the civilian in charge of the slaves' work. The officer told the civilian to put Ned to work. If Ned did not work hard enough, the civilian should tie him up and give him twenty lashes.

Giving Emma a pick ax, a shovel, and a huge wheelbarrow, the civilian sent her to help build a parapet, or barrier wall. Because she had never done this kind of work, she tried to copy the other slaves as they broke up gravel and shoveled it into a wheelbarrow. Emma became more and more tired as she pushed the wheelbarrow up a steep plank to the top of an eight-foot high wall. She almost tumbled off the wall, but some of the slaves caught her before she fell. While she ate with the other slaves at the end of the day, Emma drew sketches of the rebel defenses and listed the number of weapons she saw. She then hid both the drawing and the list under the inner sole of her shoe.

She knew she could not continue to shovel the next

day because her hands were blistered from her wrists to her fingertips. She started to look for someone to trade jobs with and found a young slave about the same size as herself. The boy, whose job was to carry water to the soldiers, agreed to trade jobs. Thanks to the young slave, Emma's second day went much better. She had to take water to only one brigade. While she served them, she asked the rebel soldiers about the number of reinforcements they expected. The next day she carried water to the slaves still working on the parapet. One of them looked at her and told her she was turning white. She tried to cover the situation by saying that she had always expected to find some white on her because her mother was white. The other slaves laughed at her and went back to work. As soon as she could, Emma found a mirror, saw the truth of what the slave had told her, and applied some more silver nitrate.

That night she went around the camp and filled the canteens with water. She overheard a peddler talking to the rebel soldiers and recognized his voice. He gave a full description of the Union camps and forces and bragged that he had revealed a Yankee lieutenant's location to some other Confederate troops, who had killed the Union officer. Emma added this piece of news to the information she would carry back to the Union generals. Emma now realized the peddler was a spy. She later wrote, "He was a fated man from that moment; his life was not worth three cents in Confederate scrip."

On the third night in the rebel camp, Ned and other slaves carried food and water to the guards. Emma gave extra food to some black guards and then stayed behind the lines instead of going back to camp with the other slaves. As heavy artillery fire from the Federal troops came from across the way, a Confederate officer came to check on the guards. He wanted to know why Ned was not back in the camp. One of the pickets who had received extra food protected Emma by telling the officer that Ned had just brought food to them. Now he had to wait for a break in the firing before he could return to camp. The Confederate officer ordered Ned to follow him. He took Emma further down the picket line, where he told another officer, "Put this fellow on the post where that man was shot until I return." Handing Emma a rifle, the officer said to shoot anything or anybody that approached from the other side. Emma later wrote about that night:

> I was all alone now, but how long before the officer might return with some one to fill my place I did not know, and I thought the best thing I could do was to make good use of the present moment. After ascertaining as well as possible the position of the picket on each side of me, each of whom I found to be enjoying the shelter of the nearest tree, I deliberately and noiselessly stepped into the darkness, and was soon gliding swiftly through the forest toward the 'land of the free,' with my splendid rifle grasped tightly lest I should lose the prize.

Because Emma did not want to get close enough to be shot by Union pickets, she lay on the ground the rest of the night. At dawn she raised a small white cloth as a signal to the Yankee guards, who allowed her to enter the camp.

Emma went straight to General George B. McClellan, who did not recognize her. He truly believed her to be a slave and ordered Ned to go tell Frank to report to him in an hour. Emma went to her tent, rubbed chalk on her face and hands, and then returned to General McClellan as Frank. She gave the general a full report of what she had learned behind the Southern lines. The general congratulated Frank on a successful mission. He sent the rebel rifle to Washington as a war memento to display in the Capitol.

Emma next planned to disguise herself as an Irish female peddler. She would pretend to follow the army to sell cakes and pies to the soldiers. She packed her clothes and props in a cake and pie basket. Then she crossed the Chickahominy River on horseback because the bridges had not been completed. She reached the other side and sent the horse back across the river to a waiting soldier. All of the contents in her basket had become soaked when she crossed the river. That night Emma had only a wet patchwork quilt to wrap around herself as she slept on the ground. Severe chills shook her body during the night. As her temperature rose, she talked wildly. For two days and two nights Emma suffered from fever and chills. She had no food, no medicine, and little strength. The pies and cakes needed for her disguise had all spoiled. She determined not to starve to death though. She put on her disguise, left the swamp, and headed for enemy lines. Emma hoped to present herself as a fugitive fleeing from the approaching Yankees.

She crossed the river on the third morning. By now she was desperate for something to eat. After she had walked all day, she arrived at a small, white house. Not knowing who might be inside, Emma entered quietly. There she found a dying rebel soldier lying on a straw mat. He could barely whisper, but he told her that he had developed typhoid fever and could not keep up with his company. He had crawled on hands and knees to the house in which she found him.

Emma began to care for him, pretending to be an Irish woman called Bridget. She took a great risk doing this because she would have faced a Confederate firing squad if she had been caught behind enemy lines.

The young man, Allen Hall, asked her to deliver his gold watch to a Major McKee at Richmond. He also told Emma to let the major know that Allen Hall had died peacefully. The soldier took a ring from his finger. He tried to put it on Emma's finger but was too weak to do so. He thanked Emma for her nursing care, asked her to pray with him, and then died. The exhausted Emma stayed beside the corpse until the next morning. Although she knew that the gold watch could help her get past the Confederate pickets, she decided to improve her disguise before she tried to go behind the enemy lines. She found mustard, pepper, an old pair of green spectacles, and a bottle of red ink to use in her disguise. She made a small, strong mustard plaster and put it on one side of her face until her skin blistered. Then she put on a black plaster patch and painted a red line around her eyes. She also used some ocher found in a closet to darken her complexion. She added the green glasses and pulled a hood partly over her face. She packed her basket with objects a refugee would likely carry, but she hid her pistol and some other suspicious items under all of these props. She wanted to fool the Confederates in case they searched her before they allowed her across the lines.

After she had hiked about five miles toward Richmond, Emma saw a sentry, or soldier on watch, in the distance and sat down to rest. She needed to prepare herself before she had to put her disguise to the test. She used her resting time to sprinkle pepper on her handkerchief and to rub her eyes with the handkerchief to make herself cry. She looked in a small mirror to make sure she looked as if she had been crying for a long time. She then approached the guard, holding a small truce flag—a piece of a cotton window curtain from the house she had just left. As he tried to cover his amusement at her appearance, the picket motioned her to come forward. He asked her several questions, which she answered in a thick Irish brogue.

Emma continued to dab at her eyes with the pepper-covered handkerchief, causing more tears to run down her face. The guard accepted her as a grieving widow and let her pass. He warned her not to stay long because they expected an attack soon. The Yankees had just completed the bridges over the Chickahominy River. In the camp, Emma asked for Major McKee so that she could give him Allen Hall's gold watch. Soldiers told her Major McKee had gone to set a trap for the Yankees and would not return until that evening. Emma decided that she would try to learn all that she could while she was in the camp. She had no trouble getting people to talk about the expected battle.

Major McKee returned and Emma delivered the sad news of his friend's death. She gave him Hall's watch, a small package of letters, and a lock of Hall's hair. The major cried for the loss of his friend and asked Emma to lead him and a few other soldiers back to the little house to prepare Hall's body for burial. She agreed but claimed to be too weak to walk any more. The major provided her a horse to ride. When they arrived at the house, he asked her to wait down the road. He told her to ride back to warn him and his men of the approach of any Yankees. As she later wrote: "I assented, and joyfully complied with the first part of his request . . . I turned and rode slowly down the road, but not 'seeing or hearing anything of the Yankees,' I thought it best to keep on in that direction until I did."

Emma galloped toward the Chickahominy River as soon as she was out of sight of the Confederate soldiers. She crossed the river, found a Union general, and made her report. She did not tell the general about Major McKee and his men because she wanted them to have time to bury their friend in peace.

Emma later went on one more spying mission disguised in clothes taken from captured Confederate soldiers from Kentucky. She still used the name Frank and moved through the Southern lines, pretending to hunt for butter and eggs for the rebel forces. On her first evening, she came to a village where she found a strong rebel cavalry and learned that she had stumbled upon the wedding of a Confederate captain. The officer questioned her and scolded her for not having joined the army. Because Kentucky rebels had no particular uniform, the butternut color clothes she wore identified her only as a Kentuckian, not as a soldier.

The captain insisted that Frank enlist and then offered him a reward to do so right away. If she refused, she would be soon drafted. Emma asked to have several days to consider, but the captain allowed her only two hours. He kept her under guard until she made her decision. When the captain returned to hear her answer, Emma stated that she wanted to wait to be drafted. The captain replied, "You will not have to wait for that, so you may consider yourself a soldier of the Confederacy from this hour, and subject to military discipline."

Emma hoped to find a way to escape before the cavalry unit moved out. But at daybreak she found herself galloping across the countryside right next to the captain. In a few minutes the rebel cavalry met a Federal cavalry party and soon engaged in hand-to-hand combat. In the confusion, Frank joined the Union soldiers. The officer in charge recognized Frank and signaled for Emma to stay close. This brought her face-to-face with the rebel officer who had drafted her. Emma pulled her pistol and shot off part of the man's nose and half his upper lip. The other rebel soldiers tried to get to Frank, but the arrival of Federal infantry turned the battle in the Union's favor. The Union commanding general praised Frank. Then he said that Frank could no longer serve as a spy in that area. If any of the rebel soldiers recognized him, he would be hanged on the nearest tree.

Emma Edmonds, alias Frank Thompson, suddenly disappeared from the Union army on April 19, 1863. Stories vary about the reason for her desertion. The most probable is that she had contracted malaria. After the army had denied her request for a leave-of-absence, Emma ran away. She may have feared discovery that she was a woman if she went to a hospital. When she recovered, she went back to life as a female army nurse. Later she wrote a book about her war experiences.

Emma returned to New Brunswick, Canada, after the war ended. She married L. H. Seelye, a mechanic. They moved from state to state in the United States. The couple had three children, two boys and a girl, all of whom died in childhood. The Seelyes later adopted two boys. Then in 1882, in Fort Scott, Kansas, Emma decided to apply for a veteran's pension. Since she had secretly served as a male nurse and spy, she did not know if she could get credit for her service. In 1882, Emma attended a reunion of her regiment. There she told the men with whom she had served about her disguise as Frank Thompson. They supported her and gave statements describing her brave service. Even with these letters, she still had to take care of the matter of

Frank Thompson's desertion from the army. She finally got the charge of desertion removed from her records. In July, Congress granted a monthly pension of $12 to Sarah E. E. Seelye, alias Frank Thompson.

Emma then moved to La Porte, Texas. In her later years she suffered repeated malaria attacks and paralysis. Just before her death on September 5, 1898, she became the only woman accepted as a regular member of the Grand Army of the Republic. After she died, Emma was buried with full military honors in Washington Cemetery, Lot G-26, in Houston, Texas. This lot belonged to the George B. McClellan Post of the Grand Army of the Republic. Emma was the only woman buried in that cemetery. The epitaph on her tombstone simply reads: "EMMA E. SEELY[E], ARMY NURSE."

In 1901, Colonel Frederick Schneider stated in an address to veterans of the Second Michigan:

No war ever developed so much bravery and devotion among women as did the great Civil War of 1861-1865. But none of the many instances recorded have surpassed the record for pure, unselfish patriotism and zeal for the cause of humanity, daring bravery and heroic fortitude as that of Sarah Emma Edmonds, Frank Thompson of Company F, in the summing up of whose life, find an extraordinary amount of patriotic devotion to the cause of her adopted country in the greatest crisis of its history, and nearly her whole life devoted to the alleviation of human suffering and the whole world made better from her having lived in it.

Belle Boyd, age seventeen or eighteen, in a military uniform she made after the battle of Front Royal. *(Berkeley County Historical Society)*

Chapter Two

Belle Boyd

When Belle Boyd was eleven, her parents planned a dinner party for some important guests. Belle wanted to attend, but her parents refused, telling her that she was too young for such a social function. The evening of the dinner, as the guests were rising from the table after finishing a good meal, they heard a loud ruckus outside. Suddenly the door burst open, and Belle rode into the dining room on a brown and white spotted horse. She sat firmly in the saddle and kept perfect control of the animal, looked her father in the eye, and said, "Well, my horse is old enough, isn't he?" Her embarrassed parents did not appreciate this display of Belle's determination to get her way, but she escaped punishment because the guests were amused.

Born on May 9, 1844, in Martinsburg, Virginia, Belle, the oldest of Benjamin Reed Boyd and Mary Elizabeth Glenn Boyds' eight children, was a tomboy who climbed trees and rode her horse wildly. Her quiet-spoken mother did little to control the reckless young girl. Belle attended school in Martinsburg with her brothers and sisters until the age of twelve. Then her parents sent her to Mount Washington Female College, where she completed her formal education.

She made her debut in Washington society four years later, in 1860. A year after she had come to Washington, the Civil War began and seventeen-year-old Belle returned to Martinsburg. Although not wealthy, the Boyd family had strong connections to the Confederate leadership, and her father volunteered for service in the Southern army. After he left, Belle helped raise funds to arm the Confederate soldiers.

Federal troops occupied Martinsburg on July 3, 1861, and the very next day an incident at her home drew Belle into the conflict between the North and the South.

On the Fourth of July, Yankee soldiers began to loot houses. They stole and broke fragile glass objects and personal items, hurled insults at the local Southern sympathizers, fired shots through windows, and threw furniture onto the streets. A squad of soldiers went to the Boyd house because they had heard that Belle had decorated her room with rebel flags. They intended to seize the flags and raise a Union flag over the Boyd house. A family servant removed the Confederate flags and burned them just before the soldiers reached Belle's room on the second floor.

A drunken Yankee sergeant decided to hoist the Union flag anyhow. Belle's mother yelled at the soldiers, "Men, every member of this household will die before that flag is raised over us." The sergeant cursed at Mrs. Boyd and pushed her aside when she attempted to slam the door in his face. Thinking the soldier had insulted her mother, Belle pulled out a revolver and shot him. She later said: "I could stand it no longer . . . my blood was literally boiling in my veins; I drew out my pistol and shot him. He was carried away mortally wounded and soon after expired."

Federal troops then searched the Boyd home and arrested Belle. After an investigation, Union officials ruled the killing a justifiable homicide. Belle's age and gender saved her from a prison sentence, but Union officials did post a guard at the Boyd house to prevent further problems. The bitter young woman vowed to get even by becoming a Confederate spy.

Belle's first opportunity to be a spy came when a reporter for the *New York Tribune* stayed at the Boyd house. The reporter met daily with Union officials to get briefings on the army's plans. Belle listened to these reports and sent the important information to the South. She later reported, "Whatever I heard I regularly and carefully committed to paper, and whenever an opportunity offered I sent my secret dispatch to some brave officer in command of the Confederate troops."

She did not use a code or even try to disguise her handwriting in the messages at first. By autumn 1861, she had joined the Confederate Intelligence as a messenger for Generals Pierre Beauregard and Stonewall Jackson. Belle had excellent horsemanship skills and wide knowledge of the Shenandoah Valley. She was able to get through the Union lines and to deliver messages to the Confederate generals. She also stole pistols, sabers, and ammunition from Union soldiers and passed these on to the South, which had a shortage of weapons. Union officers searched everywhere for their arms, never suspecting that she had sneaked them to the Confederacy.

Toward the end of 1861, the Union started to notice Belle's activities when they picked up a message written in her handwriting and signed "Belle." At the Union headquarters she faced a group of Federal officers who read the Articles of War to her and emphasized that the penalty for spying was death. They scolded her and released her because they did not see how a seventeen-year-old girl could do any real harm.

Belle's mother thought her daughter would be safer in Front Royal, forty miles south of Martinsburg. Mrs. Boyd sent Belle to stay with relatives there. Belle did not spy very often during the winter of 1861-1862 because war activities had slowed down in the Shenandoah Valley. She did come close to getting picked up by Union soldiers when she, a cousin, and a friend, both Confederate soldiers, had gone horseback riding. Belle lost control of her horse when it bolted toward a Union-held area. Because the two rebels knew that the Federal soldiers would not hurt her, they fled before the Yankees could capture them.

When Belle requested permission to return to Rebel territory, two Federal officers led her toward the Southern line. As they moved along, they referred to her companions as "cowardly rebels." These comments angered Belle, and she decided to get even, despite their having brought her to safety. Knowing where her friends waited for her, Belle took the officers right to them. She told the two young men, "Here are two prisoners that I have brought you." She introduced the surprised Federal soldiers to her two "cowardly rebels." Confederate officers released the Union soldiers within an hour.

A Union general gave Belle a travel pass when she requested permission to return to Martinsburg. But another Union officer appeared with a warrant and arrested her before the train could pull out of the station. He removed her from the train to Martinsburg and placed her on one headed to Baltimore. Belle waved a small Confederate flag out the train window throughout the whole trip to Baltimore. She was taken to the Eutaw Hotel, one of the city's finest, and treated like a celebrity. After a week, Union officials sent her to Martinsburg. They did not know what to do with her, but they did keep her under closer watch.

She arrived in Martinsburg and asked a Union provost marshal to give her a travel pass to Richmond. He agreed. On the train ride, Belle granted an interview to a *New York Tribune* reporter, who later wrote, "She pleads guilty to nearly all the charges against her, as far as they refer to conveying information to the enemy, carrying letters and parcels from the rebels within our lines to those without, and performing acts of heroic daring worthy of the days of the Revolution."

Belle returned to Front Royal and began to spy again.

She first managed to charm "Captain K." He fell in love with Belle and wrote her poems and sent flowers. He also supplied her with information. From the captain she learned about a Union council of war to be held in the drawing room of her aunt's previous home. Belle knew the layout of the house well. She remembered a bore hole in the floor of a bedroom closet just above the drawing room. Belle hid in the closet and placed her ear to the hole as the meeting began. She listened to the entire meeting, which lasted until one o'clock in the morning.

From her eavesdropping, Belle learned that General James Shields planned to take most of his Union troops out of Front Royal in the spring of 1862. They would go to support General George McClellan in his intended assault on Richmond. The Federal troops that remained in Front Royal would have little chance against a Confederate attack. Belle wrote a coded report of all that she had heard. Then she saddled her horse in preparation to deliver the message to General Turner Ashby. When Federal guards stopped her, she showed them travel passes she had secured from Confederate soldiers. No one seemed to wonder why a young woman was out riding in the moonlight at two o'clock in the morning, and she delivered the note successfully.

Belle remained in Front Royal while Major Tyndale and a small regiment still occupied the town. When Belle became bored by the lack of excitement, she, her cousin Alice, and Belle's maid Eliza decided to go to Winchester to visit friends. They requested a travel pass from Major Tyndale, who agreed to get one to them the next day. That morning their carriage appeared at the door. The girls waited for the pass to arrive. When it did not come, they learned that Major Tyndale had not issued the pass but had left the area on a scouting trip. This did not stop the determined Belle. She knew they could not get past the Federal guards without a travel pass, so they needed a Union soldier to go with them.

She saw a young Union officer whom she recognized. When "Lieutenant H" admitted that he was going to Winchester, she asked him to let the three girls go with him. The lieutenant at first refused, but Belle charmed him into agreement. The girls climbed into their waiting carriage and had a pleasant trip to Winchester. After staying there overnight with their friends, they planned to return to Front Royal with Lieutenant H the following day. A well-dressed man came to see Belle early that morning before the lieutenant picked them up. He gave her two bundles of letters and instructions on what to do with them. He also gave her another package which he said was not as important. Finally, he handed her a note which he said must reach General Stonewall Jackson or another Confederate general.

Belle hid the most important letters in Eliza's clothes because Federal agents rarely suspected black servants of any tricks. She wrote "Kindness of Lieutenant H" on the other packet of letters. Then she put them in a small basket looped over her arm. She carried the note for General Jackson in her hand as though it were of no importance. A servant in the house had watched while the man passed the letters to Belle. He reported to the authorities what he had seen. A Union official sent a telegram to Major Tyndale, who was angry that the girls had left Front Royal without a pass from him. The major told the Union official in Winchester to arrest Belle.

Belle did not dare to try to get through the sentries without a travel pass back to Front Royal. To get her way, she again used her charms. She sent flowers to the Union provost marshal in Winchester and asked him for a pass to return to Front Royal. The provost marshal sent her the pass and a thank you note for the flowers. Belle did not yet know that Major Tyndale had ordered her arrest.

The girls joined Lieutenant H for the return trip to Front Royal. Just outside Winchester, Federal detectives halted the carriage. They arrested Belle on suspicion of carrying papers to Confederate officers. The detectives took all three girls to Colonel Beal at Union headquarters. The colonel asked Belle if she were carrying illegal letters. Belle said that the only letters she carried were in the basket and handed the letters to the colonel. He immediately saw the note, "Kindness of Lieutenant H." Belle assured the Federal officer that the lieutenant knew nothing about the letters.

The colonel then noticed the slip of paper Belle was holding in her hand. It was the note that she was to deliver to General Jackson! Claiming that it was only a scrap of paper that she had picked up, the bold young woman walked toward the colonel and offered it to him. She planned to swallow the note if he actually reached for it. The colonel's anger hindered his good judgment, and he waved Belle back. He aimed his attention to poor Lieutenant H, who had just been brought in by guards. Belle regretted that she had involved the lieutenant, but she knew that she would not have otherwise escaped getting caught. The Union officials soon allowed the three girls to return home.

At Front Royal, Belle talked to the Federal officers and learned more information about the strength and location of Union forces. She realized that General Jackson should speed up his attack. This would help him save the Front Royal bridges, which the Union planned to burn as they withdrew. On May 23, 1862, General Jackson's troops approached Front Royal. Belle, dressed in a dark blue dress and a fancy white apron, ran as fast as she could across the gap between the two armies. Waving her white bonnet and shouting, she ignored the bullets that sprayed the ground all around her. Gasping for breath, she reached the Confederate side and delivered her message.

No one knows whether Belle's message affected the success of the Confederate attack, but General Jackson and his troops did save the Front Royal bridges as they advanced toward Harper's Ferry. Belle later said that after the victory, General Stonewall Jackson wrote to her: "Miss Belle Boyd, I thank you, for myself and for the army for the immense service you have rendered your country today. Hastily, I am your friend, T. J. Jackson, C.S.A."

On July 29, 1862, only a few months after Belle's

eighteenth birthday, Union officials again arrested her on suspicion of spying. They sent her to Old Capitol Prison in Washington. William Wood, the superintendent of the prison, welcomed her when she arrived: "And so this is the celebrated rebel spy. I am very glad to see you, and will endeavor to make you as comfortable as possible, so whatever you wish for, ask for it, and you shall have it. I am glad to have so distinguished a personage for my guest. Come, let me show you to your room." He then took her to prison cell number six, her room on the second floor. The room contained a washing stand, a mirror, an iron bed, a table, and some chairs. Belle requested a rocking chair and a fire to make the room more comfortable, although the hot July days did not require it. Wood provided both requests and told her he would leave her door unlocked as long as she behaved herself.

Belle received other advantages after Wood promised to make her as comfortable as possible. Admirers supplied her with many fresh foods. Instead of the usual prison fare, she enjoyed soup, beef steak, chicken, boiled corn, tomatoes, Irish stew, potatoes, bread and butter, cantaloupes, peaches, pears, and grapes. Belle learned that several guards on each floor enforced the rule that prisoners could not talk to one another. But she did not let prison sadden her. She even tried to cheer up the Confederate soldiers in prison with her by singing "Maryland, My Maryland."

Belle was a beautiful spy, but not always the smartest one. She met a fellow prisoner named Kerbey, a boy younger than herself. Although he wore a Confederate uniform, Kerbey was actually a Union spy. He had been arrested by mistake as he carried out his role as a Secret Service agent. Belle helped him plan his "escape" from Old Capitol Prison. They decided to disguise him as the black man who brought food to the prisoners. Belle made Kerbey some clothes similar to those worn by the food server. She then got a piece of burnt cork so that he could blacken his face and hands. She shared with him an escape route and described the safe houses between Washington and Richmond. Although the soldier pretended to side with Belle, he planned to give all of this information to the Union. Before his escape could take place, the secretary of war ordered Kerbey's release.

When a detective came to the prison, he tried to get Belle to pledge her loyalty to the Union. Belle refused and told him: "I hope that when I commence the oath of allegiance to the United States Government, my tongue may cleave to the roof of my mouth; and that if I ever sign one line that will show [that] I owe the United States Government the slightest allegiance, I hope my arm may fall paralyzed by my side." Union officials had never filed charges against Belle. On August 29, 1862, they released her and sent her to Richmond, where she was welcomed as a heroine. She then returned to Martinsburg and bragged to friends: "My progress through the Southern states was one long ovation. The people gathered in vast numbers to get a glimpse of the 'rebel spy.'"

Federal troops occupied Martinsburg again after the battle at Gettysburg, and once again Belle became a possible danger to them. In late summer 1863, Union officials arrested her for the second time and took her to Old Capitol Prison. There she suffered from a severe case of typhoid fever. After Belle had recovered in December, the Union sent her to the South with orders not to return for the rest of the war.

Belle started her final mission for the Confederacy after she rebuilt her strength. She left for England in May 1864, a trip she pretended was to improve her health. In reality she carried messages from the Confederate secretary of state to supporters in England. Belle boarded the *Greyhound*, a blockade-running ship, but the United States Navy captured the ship before it could cross the international border.

A young ensign, Samuel Hardinge, boarded the ship to take it back to a United States port. En route, Belle flirted with the ensign, who fell in love with her. He allowed the *Greyhound's* Confederate captain to escape, resulting in Hardinge's court-martial. Union officials took Belle prisoner once again. Rather than return to prison, Belle asked to go to Canada. Federal officials granted her permission, but told her that if she were caught in the United States, she would be shot. She traveled to London after several months in Canada. When Belle arrived there, she told the Confederacy's agent that she had destroyed the messages she carried when Union officials seized the blockade runner. This report ended Belle's service to the Confederacy.

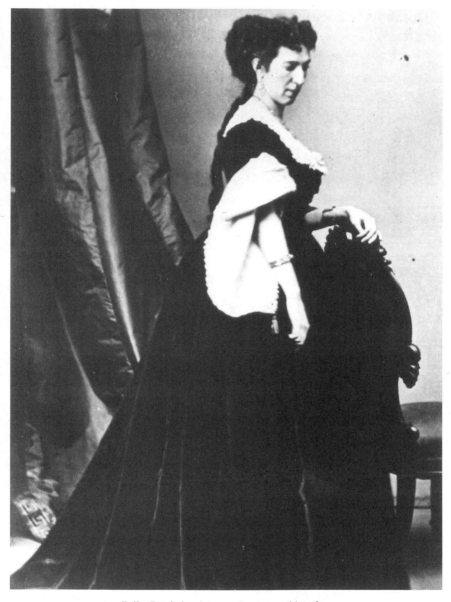

Belle Boyd the actress, about age thirty-four.
(Berkeley County Historical Society)

The former Ensign Hardinge followed her to London after his court-martial. They married in St. James Church in Piccadilly on August 15, 1864. Federal agents arrested Hardinge as a traitor to the Union when he returned to the United States. Upon his release in February 1865 from Old Capitol Prison, he set out to join Belle in England. He returned to her in poor health and died within a year. Belle found herself a penniless, pregnant widow at the age of twenty.

Belle wrote a two-volume book about her war adventures and personal life. She thought about turning the events of her book into a dramatic reading because she needed a more dependable source of income to support herself and her baby daughter, Grace. When a friend in London encouraged Belle to pursue her interest in theater performance, Belle appeared on stages to tell about her deeds as a Confederate spy. She charmed the English, and their newspaper stories stretched the truth about her bravery and importance. In 1866, President Andrew Johnson signed his Proclamation of Amnesty, allowing Belle to return home. She and her baby returned to the United States, where she took the name Nina Benjamin and continued her stage career. She gave her last performance in New Orleans at the age of twenty-five.

On March 17, 1869, in New Orleans, Belle married an Englishman and former Union officer, John Swainston Hammond. He traveled as a sales representative for a coffee and tea company. As the wife of a wealthy businessman, Belle enjoyed visits to most of the major United States cities. But the marriage was not a happy one, and Belle and John divorced in 1884. The couple had four children: Arthur, who died in infancy, Byrd, Marie Isabelle, and John Edmund.

Only six weeks after their divorce, forty-one-year-old Belle married again. Her new husband was Nathaniel Rue High Jr., a handsome young actor from Toledo, Ohio. When the uncertain income of her twenty-four-year-old husband could not support the couple, Belle began to tour again. In mostly second-rate theaters, she gave dramatic speeches about her experiences during the war. She started to emphasize the union of the North and the South, telling audiences that she never thought of herself as a spy. She had just wanted to help her people. Belle ended most of her speeches with "One God, One Flag, One People Forever," words that gained approval from survivors of both sides.

Belle wrote to her daughters just before she went on stage in Evansville, Wisconsin, on Sunday, June 10, 1900. "I feel like a criminal not sending you money. But I have only been able to play one night, and sent you all I had . . . over expenses, 2.00." The next morning she died of a heart attack at the age of fifty-six. The woman's auxiliary of the Grand Army of the Republic raised the money for her funeral. Four Union veterans lowered Belle's coffin into the grave. They had apparently accepted her "one people" slogan.

Pauline Cushman
(Library of Congress)

Chapter Three

Pauline Cushman

Yankee spy Pauline Cushman was born Harriet Wood in New Orleans, Louisiana, on June 10, 1833. Harriet's mixed heritage included Spanish, French and African ancestry. Her father lost all of his money when Harriet was ten years old and moved the family to the frontier town of Grand Rapids, Michigan. Harriet loved the outdoors and could ride horseback, hunt, shoot, canoe, and play sports as well as any boy. From this wild outdoor life, she developed a love of adventure that would last her a lifetime.

Throughout their childhood, Harriet and her seven brothers had endured their father's violent temper. One day Harriet interfered in the ongoing trouble between her demanding father and her quiet mother. A family argument followed, and at age eighteen, Harriet decided to leave home to scc the world. With only a few dollars in her purse, she went to New York, where she called on several stage managers. Her high spirits and bubbling personality caught the attention of one of them, who made her an offer to appear in a theater in New Orleans, her birthplace. Her career as an actress had begun, and she changed her name to Pauline Cushman.

Pauline, who enjoyed noisy, flashy roles in which she could sing loud, rousing songs, was in Union-held Louisville, Kentucky, when war broke out in 1861. She had a part in *The Seven Sisters*, a road show at Woods Theater. Her dark coloring, flashing eyes, full rosy lips, and long, shiny black hair charmed her audiences. One night two Confederate officers approached Pauline and offered her $300 to toast Southern President Jefferson Davis during her performance. After begging for time to consider their proposal, she rushed to inform Colonel Moore, the Federal provost marshal. The marshal saw a chance to use Pauline as a spy. If she made the toast, she would appear to support the South. This would provide her entry to Confederate camps and make her valuable to the Union. The action appealed both to her patriotism and to her sense of adventure, and Pauline agreed. The marshal asked her to take the oath of allegiance to insure her loyalty to the Union.

On the night of the proposal, Pauline stepped to the front of the stage in the middle of the performance. She raised the glass in her hand and shouted: "Here's to Jeff Davis and the Southern Confederacy. May the South always maintain her honor and her rights!" After a shocked silence, the audience broke into jeers and cheers, depending upon their loyalties. Then fights erupted. The theater company fired Pauline, and Union officials "arrested" her, holding her just long enough to fool the Confederates. She became a heroine overnight. Southerners believed in her loyalty to the South and told her about blockade running, counter spying, and other Southern operations behind Union lines. Pauline took all of the information straight to the Federal provost marshal.

Federal officials then pretended to throw her out of Union territory, and she began to follow the Confederate army. She claimed to be looking for her "lost" brother, a rebel soldier. She had no trouble getting information about enemy defenses and operations from soldiers who adored her. She gathered lists of those who opposed the Union, including any Confederate spies she could identify. Pauline spent a great deal of time on horseback as a Union messenger in Kentucky, Tennessee, northern Georgia, Alabama, and Mississippi. Her knowledge of back roads and small towns helped her guide the Union troops. This information gave them an advantage over the rebels. As she traveled, she discovered several ways the Confederates sent concealed letters across the lines. She learned that farmers' wives folded messages in half lengthwise and stuffed them down chickens' throats. The women also hid messages in the handles of farmers' butter knives and in packages of flour.

Pauline's activities caught the attention of Federal Colonel William Truesdail. He managed the Army police, which included a large network of spies. In their first conference, Truesdail told her he had a hard assignment for her that would require a great deal of courage. Even though he said that it could lead to glory or end in death, she urged him to give her more information. The colonel wanted Pauline to visit the five camps of Confederate General Braxton Bragg. He believed that Pauline would have no trouble getting into the camps because of her beauty and her reputation as a Southern supporter.

They decided on a plan for Pauline's arrival in a camp: When she reached enemy picket lines, she should show her papers. She should then request a meeting with the camp's commanding officer, whom she would tell about her desire to find her brother somewhere in the Confederate army. She would ask the officer to give her help and protection as well as a letter to get her safely to the next camp. She should accept all invitations to ride through the camps. As she rode, she should notice details of defenses and weapons. She must not ask questions about the military, but she could ask to visit the sick and wounded. At the hospitals she could ask the doctors if they had enough medical supplies. She could also inquire about the source of their supplies and the number of sick and wounded. She must *never* write down anything. As an actress, Pauline had learned to memorize. She would now use that ability in her spying activities.

The Union sent Pauline out of Nashville in May 1863, shortly before her thirtieth birthday. They placed her in a closed carriage that took her beyond the Federal lines. Three miles outside of Nashville, the colonel's servant waited for her with a magnificent bay horse, which she mounted and galloped away. After she had ridden for a while across a "neutral" area, Pauline needed to cross a river. A few burned planks were all that remained of the bridge, but she saw a pathway that she hoped would lead to a spot where she could ford the river.

She came upon a house and asked to spend the night. The smuggler who lived there agreed to take her across the Confederate lines in a buggy if she would sell him her horse and saddle for $100 in Confederate money. Having little choice, Pauline agreed. The next morning the smuggler took her to Columbia, Tennessee, where he left her at the Franklin Hotel. Pauline soon found out how much the smuggler had cheated her on the horse and saddle. A breakfast of hoe cakes without butter, coffee made of rye, and a small amount of fat bacon cost her $8.00 at the hotel.

After she arrived in Columbia, Pauline made two new friends among the Federal officers, Major Boone and Captain P. A. Blackman. When she told them that she needed to move on to the next camp at Shelbyville, Tennessee, the major gave her a letter to introduce her to the next officer. She thanked him and told him she would return to see him after she found her brother. Pauline headed for Shelbyville, where she took a hotel room. As she sat in the hotel dining room and observed the other diners, she selected her contact, a serious young engineer who sat at the next table drawing plans of rebel defenses. Pauline used her letter from Major Boone as an introduction. She soon won the young man's trust. He even offered her his own letter of introduction to General Bragg, which she accepted. The engineer said that he must go to his desk downstairs in order to write the letter. He excused himself and left her alone with the plans. Pauline grabbed some of the blueprints and slipped them into her dress.

She carried the plans with her when she left Shelbyville. Although she had not seen General Bragg, she had met many other officers who had given her tours of their defenses and explained in detail about war preparations, weapons, and medical supplies. Pauline had too much information to memorize it all, and she ignored her earlier instructions never to carry any written papers. She thought no one would discover her "perfect hiding place" for her notes when she hid them between the inner and outer cork soles of her extra pair of boots.

Captain Blackman was glad to see her when she returned to Columbia and asked her to become his aide-de-camp, or assistant military officer. He even ordered a complete gray uniform made for her. She agreed to wear the uniform after she had made a trip back to Nashville. She stuffed the uniform in a small bag and went in search of the smuggler who had earlier helped her across Confederate lines. When she found him again, Pauline sensed a new lack of friendliness from the smuggler. She did not realize that he feared she would reveal his double-dealing activities. Pauline tried to find another way to get across the lines and had almost convinced the smuggler's son to "borrow" his father's horse so that she could escape.

Before she could leave the cabin, a Confederate scout walked in the back door. He demanded to see her pass and told her that General Bragg had issued orders to arrest anyone trying to leave Southern territory without a pass. She realized the smuggler had double-crossed her. The scout took her from the cabin so fast that she had no time to grab her bag containing her shoes with the notes. But the scout failed to search her and did not find her gun. He put her on a borrowed horse and rode in front of her through the woods. Plans to save herself raced through her mind. Then her hand touched the hidden gun. One shot could free her. She pointed the gun at the scout's back. Then over his shoulder, the man made a kind remark to her. The pistol dropped to her side; she could not shoot him in cold blood.

Pauline spent some nervous hours at scout headquarters at Anderson's Mill waiting the arrival of Brigadier General John Hunt Morgan. He said that he must hold her as a prisoner of war until he could report her case to General Bragg. He also would not let her return to the smuggler's cabin to get the bag she had left behind. Then a well-known rebel scout, Duval McNairy, came to accompany her southward. They rested for a while in a farmer's house in Hillsboro, Tennessee. Pauline decided to take matters into her own hands. She paid a black man to start a rumor that the Yankees were approaching Hillsboro. In the confusion that followed, she grabbed a horse and started toward the Union lines.

She had to pass six rebel sentries to get there, but she knew the password, "a friend." She had also discovered the countersign, "Jeff Davis and the Southern Confederacy," and she passed the first five guards. When she reached the sixth picket, her luck ran out. The older guard refused to let her through without a written pass. Pauline tried every way she knew to bribe him, but the guard held her at the line until four rebel scouts arrived and arrested her.

The scouts brought her to the fierce-tempered General Nathan Bedford Forrest. He greeted her: "Miss Cushman, I'm glad to see you. You're pretty sharp at turning a card, but I think we've got you on this last shuffle, and I've made up my mind not to part with you during the war."

That night Forrest placed a guard outside Pauline's tent. She tried to crawl out through a small opening. As she began to exit, she saw a sharp sword held just above her breast. Forrest himself had caught her as he walked around the camp. He ordered a change of guard and told a squad of men to move closer to her tent. She had to listen all night to their stories about the rebels' cruel treatment of Yankee prisoners. The next morning General Forrest ordered Pauline to be taken to General Bragg in Shelbyville. By this time, exhaustion and lack of sleep had made her too weak to walk or to ride a horse. Forrest provided an ambulance to carry her. As she prepared to leave the camp, Yankee soldiers stared at her. One of them remarked upon her beauty, but his companion responded, "She might be as beautiful as a Venus, but I would hang her on the highest tree."

At last Pauline met the famous General Bragg, a small man with dark, gray eyes and iron-gray hair and whiskers. He glanced over her papers and then began to question her. When he learned that she had been born in New Orleans, the general commented on her "Yankee twang." She replied that she had played Yankee roles in the theater for so long, she must have picked up the accent. Bragg asked her about the charges the Union had brought against her. She told him how she had made the toast to Jefferson Davis from the stage in Woods Theater. Bragg wanted to know why she had not brought the rebels such scarce articles as quinine and other malaria medicines. She replied that Federal agents had seized her supplies. Bragg continued to ask questions about the Union to which he already knew the answers, hoping to catch Pauline giving the wrong responses. When he finished his questioning, he turned her over to Colonel McKinstry, the provost marshal, to continue the investigation.

As a guard led her away, Pauline asked Bragg what would happen to her if they found her guilty. He replied, "If found guilty, you will be hanged." She begged the general to shoot her rather than hang her if she must die. She told him: "General, come now! I don't think I'd be either useful or ornamental dangling at the end of a rope."

When they reached his office, the provost marshall showed Pauline the Confederate uniform he had found in her satchel. He observed that it would have been an excellent disguise for a spy. He asked her where she got it. For once, Pauline decided to tell the truth. She explained how Captain Blackman had asked her to be his aide-de-camp. When she took from her pocket the captain's letter requesting her to be his aide, the provost marshal ordered the immediate arrest of the captain. Then he pulled from his desk the papers that Pauline had hidden in her boots. At that moment she wished she had followed instructions not to carry notes. When she admitted to the provost marshal that she recognized the papers, he questioned her about the sketches. She laughed and pretended the drawings were just guess-work to entertain herself. The provost marshal finally sent Pauline away but remarked to himself as she left the room, "That woman is the very devil, and would almost convince one that black was white!"

During June 1863, Pauline stayed in a private home while she waited to learn her fate. She became friendly with another officer. Twenty-seven-year-old Captain S.E. Pedden fell in love with the beautiful thirty-year-old woman. He ignored the fact that Captain Blackman was now in jail because he too had loved her. Pauline did not want the extra attention and favors that Captain Pedden gave her, but she felt too weak to protest. Ten days passed. Pauline waited for the decision from the hearing. Even Captain Pedden dared not tell her anything about the progress of the trial. Then he brought the terrible judgment to her. Pedden knelt by her side, took her hand, and told her to prepare herself for the worst. The court had condemned her to death. The sentence of death did not bother her as much as the means of death. She screamed and fell back on her pillow when she heard that she would be hanged as a spy.

A few days later, rumors spread that Union forces were near Shelbyville. By this time, ill health and the fear of her hanging had weakened Pauline even more. She listened to the sounds of the approaching troops. As the gunfire continued, most of the scared rebels fled the town, leaving Pauline behind. Captain Pedden kissed her goodbye and promised to look for her after the war ended. Then he too fled. Pauline wrapped herself in a blanket and stood on the balcony to greet the Federal troops when they arrived.

Pauline wanted to get away from the scene of her near hanging, but she remained weak. Union General Robert S. Granger ordered an ambulance to take her to Nashville. On that rainy day in June, Generals Granger and Mitchell carried her down from her room in a chair. Major Fullerton held an umbrella over her head. In Nashville, Pauline continued to suffer from a deep sadness. Large tears often rolled down her pale face. To try to cheer her, Union officials found a room for her in a private home instead of in a hotel. Many of the Union officers visited her and treated her like a favorite sister.

Generals Granger and James A. Garfield appointed her a major of cavalry. They recognized her brave service to the Union and the suffering she had endured. Some Nashville women made her an expensive Union-blue riding outfit trimmed in military style. From that

Pauline Cushman's autograph became valuable after she was appointed major of cavalry.

time on, soldiers called her "Major Pauline Cushman." After she regained her health, crowds flocked to see the brave Union spy and begged for her autograph.

In 1864, Pauline published *The Thrilling Adventures of Pauline Cushman,* a book about her spying activities. She then began a tour of the country to tell about her experiences, embellishing the stories each time she told them. Her book generated so much interest that people filled theaters to see her in person. The flashy Pauline did not disappoint them. Wearing fancy clothes and carrying big bouquets of roses in her arms, she exaggerated everything she did. After a time though, people in the South lost interest, and the theater crowds dwindled. She then extended her acting roles toward the west, arriving in California in 1872. When she could no longer get acting jobs in San Francisco, Pauline turned to sewing for a living. She became addicted to morphine because of severe arthritis pain. On the morning of December 2, 1893, Pauline's landlady found her unconscious in the boarding house. Sixty years old,

Pauline died later that afternoon of a heart attack, perhaps brought on by an intentional overdose of morphine.

The Women Relief Corps of the San Francisco Grand Army of the Republic provided a splendid funeral with a large white coffin covered in thousands of white flowers. Pauline was buried with full military honors—flags, honor guard, and rifle salutes—on December 6, 1893. Her body was placed in the officers' circle at the National Cemetery in Presidio. Her gravestone gives only her name and the title "Union Spy."

Pauline Cushman's name is not connected to any specific Federal military successes, but the Union held her service in the highest regard as seen in this *New York Times* excerpt from May 28, 1864: ". . . among the women of America who have made themselves famous since the opening of the rebellion, few have suffered more or rendered more service to the Federal cause than Pauline Cushman, the female scout and spy."

Rose O'Neal Greenhow and her daughter, Rose, in the Old Capitol Prison.
(Library of Congress)

Chapter Four

Rose O'Neal Greenhow

Twelve-year-old Rose O'Neal's dark hair streamed behind her as her horse galloped across the landscape. Throwing her head back and laughing with joy, she ignored the unwritten rule that a Southern lady should not show her legs. Instead she rode with her sashed muslin dress and white apron bunched around the saddle horn. She bent her limber body across the horse's neck and spurred it to go faster. People said that Rose had inherited her delight in riding horses from her father, a wealthy landowner who had died when she was just a baby. In her teen years, Rose was a tall young woman with long legs and a slim waist. Her flashing black eyes, sparkling white teeth, and flushed olive skin earned her the nickname "Wild Rose."

Rose and her older sister, Ellen Elizabeth, went to Washington in 1833 when Rose was sixteen. They visited their aunt, Mrs. Hill, who operated the Congressional Boarding House in the Old Capitol Building.

Aunt Hill kept the two girls busy, learning social graces and attending well-chaperoned parties. Rose's love for this social life would blossom later when she would become a Washington hostess.

At twenty-six years of age, Rose married Dr. Robert Greenhow, a handsome Virginia lawyer, seventeen years her senior. The couple had three daughters—Florence, Gertrude, and Leila. In 1850, Dr. Greenhow saw a great opportunity to leave Washington and become a law officer for the United States Land Commission on the West Coast. Although Rose did not want to leave Washington, she followed her husband to San Francisco. She and the girls later returned for a visit to Washington with her new daughter, little Rose. While Rose was gone, Robert fell off a raised sidewalk in San Francisco. Although he stood up and walked on, he started to suffer great pain and died six weeks later.

With four children ranging from an infant to a teenager, Rose could not make the difficult trip to attend her husband's funeral. She and her daughters moved into the house that her husband had left her at 398 16th Street in Washington, D.C. This address would later become the Confederacy's spy headquarters in Washington. Rose had announced her support for the South before the Civil War began: "I am a Southern woman, born with Revolutionary blood in my veins."

Rose counted Senator Henry Wilson of Massachusetts, chairman of the Senate Military Affairs Committee, among her close friends. He wrote love letters to Rose and signed them with an "H." "You will know that

I love you and will sacrifice anything," he wrote in one letter. In another, he promised: "Tonight, at whatever cost I will see you . . . I will be with you tonight, and then I will tell you again and again that I love you." Such devotion would later help Rose in her role as a Confederate spy. Although Senator Wilson did not betray the Union on purpose, the beautiful widow had little trouble getting information from him.

Rose's deep voice, her gift for conversation, and her strong political views attracted people of all kinds to her home. Politicians and society's leaders all wanted invitations to her dinners. The charming hostess asked clever questions and listened with care to get information. She sent all that she learned to the Confederacy.

When the war broke out, she joined the Confederacy's spy efforts led by Lieutenant Colonel Thomas Jordan of Virginia. Jordan had developed an elaborate Washington spy network that included three espionage rings. Jordan became interested in Rose because of her connection to Senator Wilson. Rose became the leader of one ring and went to work with enthusiasm. She used "every capacity with which God endowed [her]."

She learned how to use a simple twenty-six-symbol code Jordan had invented. Rose also took advantage of her social connections with important Union figures. She continued to talk and dance with men, charming them with her conversational skills and beauty to make them reveal important information. After putting into code the details of the information she gained, she sent it to Confederate officers.

Rose helped the Confederate cause most when she obtained critical information before the battle at Manassas. On July 10, 1861, she contacted Betty Duvall, one of her agents. She needed Betty to take a message to General Pierre Beauregard at Fairfax Court House near Bull Run. Rose wrote the coded message on a tiny sheet of paper: "McDowell [General Irwin] has certainly been ordered to advance on the sixteenth. ROG" She sewed the message inside a small, black silk pouch about the size of a silver dollar, which Betty Duvall hid in her tightly-wound black hair.

Betty wore a rough gray dress to disguise herself as a market man's daughter. She left Washington in a farmer's wagon and then spent the night in Virginia. There she changed into a stylish riding outfit and continued toward Fairfax Court House. Pickets, or soldiers who stood watch to look for enemies, stopped Betty as she neared Fairfax and took her to General Milledge L. Bonham, a South Carolina congressman. Making sure that Beauregard got the exact message, Betty took out her combs and unwound her long black hair to reveal the silk packet. The beautiful brunette's sparkling black eyes, perfect features, and patriotic glow impressed the general. He quickly sent Beauregard the message, giving him a chance to strategically rearrange his troops. Although Betty had successfully completed her task, she was too beautiful to continue as a spy. Once a man had seen her, he would not likely forget her face.

The Southern generals needed more information. They sent George Donellan, a Confederate soldier, to

Washington, where he introduced himself to Rose by showing her the coded words, "Trust Bearer." The message to Rose read: "Yours was received at 8 o'clock at night. Let them come. We are ready for them. We rely upon you for precise information. Be particular as to description and destination of force, quantity of artillery, etc." Her return message stated that McDowell would advance to Manassas with 55,000 Union soldiers. Donellan hid her reply in the heel of one of his boots and returned to the Confederate generals.

Rose had another message for Donellan to deliver on July 17. She had learned about the Union's plan to cut off the Manassas Gap that led into the valley. This action could prevent General Joe Johnston from joining forces with General Beauregard. Her early warning allowed the Confederate soldiers to move through the gap and be in place when General McDowell and his troops arrived.

McDowell believed he had more soldiers than the South, but he had a deep concern about the lack of experience of his young troops. Others showed great confidence in the Union. They believed that once they were organized, they could fight one decisive battle and end the war. Public opinion pressured McDowell to move out. Rose saw this pressure on McDowell. Although she knew the Union had more soldiers, both trained and untrained, than the South, she believed the Union would not have the advantage if the South could know the Union route ahead of time. Rose delivered this information to the Confederacy.

Because of their confidence in a victory, Union sena-
tors and their wives rode out in carriages toward
Manassas to watch the battle from a distance, enjoying
picnic lunches packed in hampers. They watched the
soldiers that afternoon until the holiday excitement
suddenly turned to terror. The Federal troops began to
withdraw slowly at first, but then it was every man for
himself. Exhausted Union soldiers staggered along the
road, leaving their dead comrades behind. When the
retreating soldiers reached Washington, they collapsed
in the streets.

On the day of the battle, Rose went to New York to
take her second daughter, Leila, to join her older sister
Florence and her husband, who were going to California. If Rose had other reasons for being out of Washington on July 21, she never said. Because Florence's
husband was a Union supporter, Rose had to rejoice by
herself at the news of the Union loss. When she returned to Washington, Rose found a message from the
Confederacy: "Our President [Jefferson Davis] and our
General [Beauregard] direct me to thank you. We rely
upon you for further information. The Confederacy
owes you a debt."

Rose then suffered another personal tragedy. Her
third daughter, Gertrude, sickly since childhood, died.
Rose mourned the loss of her daughter but continued to
work with her agents. While they moved through Washington to gather information, Rose herself toured the
capital's defenses. She obtained a full set of blueprints
and detailed statements about the Union's military

strength. She and her agents also made plans for the possibility of approaching Confederate troops. When the guns roared a warning and all the church bells rang, she and others would take advantage of the city's panic. They would cut telegraph wires that connected forts and other Union defenses.

The expected invasion of Washington never occurred, and Union troops started to bring captured Confederate soldiers into the city. The boarding house of her aunt, Mrs. Hill, became the Old Capitol Prison. Rose visited the Confederate soldiers, carrying baskets of food and clothing to them and discouraging the rebel soldiers from taking an oath of loyalty to the Union. After Federal officials barred her from the prisons, she continued to send the prisoners food and supplies and passed along lists of their names to the Confederacy. Never making any attempt to hide her activities, Rose boasted that she had Federal men to supply her information that she sent to the South.

In 1861, the Union employed its first spy catcher, Allan Pinkerton. The short, plump-faced, forty-one-year-old Chicago detective had as much love for the Union as Rose had for the Confederacy. His job was to discover the traitors in Washington and to put an end to spying in the city. Pinkerton had heard stories about Rose. He placed guards at her two-story brick house to identify every person who entered or left her home. His agents then investigated each of those persons. One day Pinkerton noticed something different about the Greenhow house. All of the shades were closed with only slits of light coming from the first floor parlor.

Pinkerton and two of his assistants decided to investigate. Because the windows were too high for him to peer through the slats of the shutters, he kicked off his boots and stood on the shoulders of his two aides. Cold, gusty winds and heavy rains interfered with their efforts. Just as Pinkerton got into place, he heard someone coming toward the house. The three men hid under a staircase that led to the front door. Pinkerton got back in place after a man went into the house, but he could only see an unoccupied, elegant room. Then the handsome man who had just gone into the house entered the parlor. Pinkerton recognized him as a captain in charge of a provost marshal's station.

The captain, who appeared troubled and restless, continued watching the door. When Rose entered the room, the captain's face glowed with pleasure. She greeted her guest and led him to a table in the rear of the room. The captain then drew out a map from an inner pocket, and the two bent over it. Pinkerton could hear only pieces of their conversation, but he heard enough to know they discussed Washington's defenses.

When the captain left the house, Pinkerton, still without his shoes, followed him through blinding mist and a driving rain. The captain then disappeared into a doorway at the corner of Pennsylvania Avenue and Fifteenth Street. Four soldiers came out of the doorway with their bayonets pointed at Pinkerton. They seized the detective and threw him into a dark cell where he spent the night—shoeless, wet, and cold.

Pinkerton managed to persuade a kind-hearted guard to let him send a message. Soon the guards released Pinkerton and arrested the captain. They placed him in a single cell. A detective questioned him continuously about the spying in Washington, especially the role of Rose Greenhow. No one else could talk to the captain, not even those who brought him food. In despair, the captain committed suicide in his cell.

Rose continued her activities as a spy for the Confederacy even after she heard about the possibility of her own arrest as one of the Union's identified "dangerous persons." She may have believed that the Union officials would never arrest a woman, or she may have thought she could outsmart all of the Yankees. In either case, she continued her spying.

Rose left her house to go for a walk on the morning of August 23, 1861. She looked down the street and saw several men staring at her. She suspected that these were Union men. As Rose continued her walk, another member of her spy ring passed by. She told the agent: "Watch from the corner. If they arrest me, I'll raise my handkerchief." Rose stopped, reached into her pocket, and crumpled a small piece of paper that contained a secret message. She then brushed her hand across her mouth and swallowed the paper. But she could not swallow the larger document that she carried. No one knows for sure what information this document contained, but Rose considered it very important.

Then she turned and strolled back to her house. Just as she reached the front door, Pinkerton stepped forward and asked if she was Mrs. Greenhow. When she nodded, he arrested her. After touching her handkerchief to her lips, Rose began to shout at Pinkerton: "I have no power to resist you. But had I been inside of my house, I would have killed you before I submitted to this illegal procedure." He ignored her rage and told her to go inside.

As they entered the house, men appeared from everywhere and started a massive search. Little eight-year-old Rose, who had observed her mother's arrest, started to shout out the door, "Mother's been arrested!" Pinkerton's men tried to stop her, but she ran outside, climbed a tree, and continued to shout the news of her mother's arrest.

Rose worried that Union agents would search her and find the other important document that she carried. She told a guard she needed to put on different clothes because she was too hot. He agreed to let her go upstairs to her bedroom to change dresses. She shut her bedroom door and pulled out the document. Just as she did so, the guard opened the door. He had regretted his decision to leave Rose alone and had followed her upstairs. He did not enter her room but stood just outside the doorway. Rose pulled out a gun, ready to shoot him if he crossed the threshold. But he stayed in the doorway, and she chewed up the document as well. She barely had time to hide the gun before a female operative entered her bedroom and searched Rose down to her underwear.

When Rose's most trusted agent, Lillie Mackell,

joined her upstairs, the two women remembered some important Confederate papers hidden in the library. Rose told Lillie they must recover the papers or they would have to burn the house down! As she waited for an opportunity to go to the library, Rose stood at a window and tried to warn other people in the spy ring to stay away from the house. A detective twisted her arm to keep her from signaling some government clerks who did not see her and came into the house, unaware of the danger. The clerks tried to convince Pinkerton they had come only for a friendly visit, but he arrested them and took them away.

After Pinkerton left, the guards started to drink from the liberal stock of liquor in the house. Their drinking spree provided Rose and Lillie an opportunity to re-cover the damaging papers. They rushed to the library, pulled the papers from a book on the shelf, and hurried back to the bedroom. When the guard came back, the two women lay on the bed. Rose did not destroy all of the rebel papers though. Always the daring spy, she decided to get one of the messages to the South. She handed the note under the sheet to Lillie and told her to put it in her stocking because the woman detective who had searched Rose had not looked at her shoes or stock-ings.

At about 3:30 a.m., detectives told Lillie that she could leave the house. The two women had made a plan that Lillie would start to cry and say that she did not want to leave her friend if the Union agents tried to search Lillie before she left. But the guards allowed her to leave with only a careless inspection. Although Union agents did follow her when she left the house, she managed to send the message to the Confederacy. The search of Rose's house continued. She later wrote that the Union agents read private letters and papers collected over a lifetime. They destroyed furniture and followed her to the bathroom, where a guard stood at the door. She declared, "They . . . subjected me to an ordeal . . . by a total disregard of the laws of decency."

Rose's house soon earned the nickname "Fort Greenhow," where she and her little girl remained under house arrest. Rose wrote to President Lincoln and requested permission to attend church, stating, "My castle has become my prison." The president denied her the request. Crowds paced back and forth in front of "Fort Greenhow," hoping to catch a glimpse of the famous spy.

Despite her imprisonment, Rose continued to be a thorn in the Union's side. She annoyed her guards and stirred up the other prisoners with her fiery speeches. She waved a Confederate flag from her bedroom window and sent coded messages to the South through a "vocabulary of colors" by hiding coded symbols among other designs in her needlepoint embroideries. Pinkerton and his men continued to keep a close watch on her, and after some time they broke the code she used.

Rose wrote letters to the newspapers and complained about her imprisonment. On January 18, 1862, Union agents moved her to a more spy-proof jail, Old Capitol Prison. She still sent letters out of this grimy, lice-

The Greenhow home was turned into a makeshift prison for women spies during the Civil War. *(Library of Congress)*

infested building by using her young daughter and the son of another prisoner. When the children went out to play, they carried the notes and gave them to trusted agents. But Rose herself could no longer serve as an effective spy from the Old Capitol Prison. She remained there about a year before the Union offered her parole on the condition that she must sign an oath promising not to aid the enemy. When Rose refused to sign, she and several other female spies were sent away to the South. Confederate President Jefferson Davis received her there on June 2, 1862. She felt that all of her efforts had been worthwhile when he told her, "But for you, there would have been no Bull Run."

The long prison sentence had made Rose nervous and excitable. She had not endured well the loneliness and silence of her cell, and it took her several months to recover. Afterwards she toured Britain and France to spread propaganda for the Confederate cause. She discovered that the ruling classes in these two countries had a strong sympathy for the South. She also published the memoirs of her imprisonment.

Rose decided to return home in 1864. She boarded the British blockade runner, the *Condor*, which was trying to avoid a Federal blockade in order to bring military and other goods into a Southern port. A Union gunboat began to pursue the *Condor* as it neared the home coastline. During the chase, the *Condor* ran aground at the mouth of Cape Fear River near Wilmington, North Carolina. Rose feared capture by the Union gunboat and begged the captain to place a lifeboat in the water for her. The captain protested because of stormy weather and huge waves. Rose insisted that she trusted the wild sea more than she trusted Yankees.

The boat overturned before she and her fellow passengers could reach shore, but all of the passengers, except Rose, washed ashore. She sank because of her heavy, black silk dress and the two thousand dollars in gold coins she carried. The money represented the royalties from her memoirs, and Rose refused to let go of her purse. She drowned on September 30, 1864. A Confederate soldier found her body washed ashore the next day, took the money, and then pushed her body back into the water. After the body again floated ashore later in the day, the owners of another blockade runner, the *Night Hawk,* identified the corpse. The ashamed soldier returned the money when he learned the identity of the body.

Sailors brought Rose's body to the Wilmington wharf, where many women lined up to receive it. Over one hundred citizens offered their houses for the funeral services, but the townsmen decided to make the ceremony public. They wrapped Rose's body in a Confederate flag and laid her out for viewing. Confederate soldiers carried the casket as the funeral procession wound its way through Wilmington's streets on October 1, 1864. Rose was buried according to the rites of the Roman Catholic Church, and soldiers fired a gun salute as others lowered her casket. Her grave marker, a marble cross, reads: "Mrs. Rose O'N. Greenhow, a bearer of dispatchs [sic] to the Confederate Government."

Elizabeth Van Lew
(Swem Library, College of William and Mary)

Chapter Five

Elizabeth Van Lew

Elizabeth Van Lew never left Richmond and never crossed any enemy picket lines. Instead she served the Union right in the heart of Confederate territory. She was a forty-three-year old spinster when she started to spy. With her small, bony figure, sharp features, and thin-lipped jaw, she had no beauty to help her gain information from the enemy. Instead she had to use her clever, inventive mind and her courage. She gained a reputation as one of the most successful spies on either side of the Civil War.

Born on October 15, 1818, Elizabeth was the oldest daughter of John Van Lew, a respected and successful hardware merchant. Her mother, Elizabeth Baker Lew, was the daughter of a former Philadelphia mayor. Elizabeth grew up in this prominent Richmond family with all of the advantages of wealth. The family lived in a grand, three-and-a-half-story mansion on Church Hill, the highest of seven hills in Richmond. The Van Lew house served as the center of Richmond's social life and featured a sixteen-foot hallway, a terraced garden, imported marble mantles, silk-covered walls, and magnificent chandeliers.

The Van Lews owned slaves, as did most other wealthy Southern families. Elizabeth had great sympathy for the slaves. In Philadelphia she attended a school that opposed slavery. After that she became even stronger in her antislavery views. She recognized that her attitude differed from that of most Richmond citizens. She said, "From the time I knew right from wrong it was my sad privilege to differ in many things from the . . . opinions and principles of my locality."

After Elizabeth's father died, she persuaded her mother and her brother John to free their nine slaves. She then bought the children of these slaves and freed them as well. Several of the Van Lew slaves chose to stay with the family as paid servants. Many of them later assisted Elizabeth in her spying activities. Her determination to fight slavery reached its peak after the hanging of John Brown, following his raid on Harper's Ferry. Because she wanted to see the nation stay together, Elizabeth sent information to Washington for two years before the war began on April 13, 1861.

Four days later, Elizabeth observed the Confederates raise their flag over Richmond. That night she watched the Confederate torchlight parade and committed herself to fight for the Union. She started to send information to her Union contacts about the number, condition, and movement of Confederate troops. After the rebels

The Van Lew Mansion was one of the largest residences in Richmond.
(Library of Congress)

defeated the Union at the Battle of Bull Run on July 21, 1861, Elizabeth asked permission to nurse the wounded Union soldiers in Richmond prisons. A Confederate provost marshal gave her a pass into Libby Prison. Elizabeth found overcrowded, filthy conditions inside the converted warehouse. She let the miserable Federal soldiers know that she came as a friend by bringing them books and small gifts such as stationery. Elizabeth used the books she brought in and out of the prison as a way to carry coded messages. Some of the books contained faintly underlined letters and numbers that formed a message when read together. Tiny pin pricks on other pages also conveyed coded messages.

Elizabeth had a special way to carry letters secretly to and from the prisoners. She used a pan with a false bottom designed to hold hot water to keep food warm. Guards must have become suspicious of how often she carried "food" in and out of the prison in this same container. One day she overheard a guard express his doubts about the pan to another guard. The next time she went to the prison, she again carried the food warming pan, but this time she had filled the bottom with boiling water instead of letters. As she tried to enter the prison, the guard asked to inspect the pan. Without hesitation she handed him the hot pan. He grabbed it with both hands and then quickly dropped it. After that experience no one again questioned her use of the pan.

Elizabeth carried both letters and messages in and out of the prison. She talked to new prisoners who told her what they had seen as they had marched from camp to camp on their way to Richmond. They told her about the strength and location of rebel troops. Elizabeth sent all of this important information to Union officers. Union prisoners also listened to the talk of their doctors, nurses, and guards. These overheard conversations became one of the greatest sources of information passed along to Elizabeth.

Newspaper articles criticized Elizabeth and her mother for their time and money spent on Union soldiers, but Elizabeth continued to serve the prisoners. She described the terrible prison conditions in her August 10, 1861, journal entry: "Sad day. Three prisoners died. The only medical attention these unfortunates get

Elizabeth Van Lew and her mother nursed wounded Union soldiers at Libby Prison in Richmond. *(Library of Congress)*

is what Mother and I give them. It is not enough. No one should see the sights I have seen. Men with limbs missing, forced to live in the filthiest of conditions. Our mare has a cleaner stall to sleep in."

To try to offset her Southern neighbors' criticism, Elizabeth pretended to be insane. She wore soiled, torn clothes and muddy shoes. Her matted, uncombed hair fell from under a ripped bonnet. As she shuffled down the street, she jerked her head back and forth, hummed aloud, and carried on imaginary conversations. If anyone tried to question her, she stared blankly ahead. This disguise fooled many people, who nicknamed her "Crazy Bet." However, it did not fool everyone. Elizabeth lived in constant danger. A *New York Times* article written after the war stated, ". . . there was not a moment during those four years [of Civil War] when Lizzie Van Lew could hear a step behind her on the street without expecting to have someone tap her on the shoulder and say, 'You are my prisoner.' "

Elizabeth became more and more involved in sending coded messages. She wrote all of them in an invisible ink that turned black with an application of milk. In the back of her watch, she carried the ciphered code she used for all of the messages. After her death, the worn, yellowed code was discovered in the place it had been hidden for forty years. One day an agent for the Pinkerton Detective Agency told her not to send such information through the post. The message might fall into the hands of Confederates who would arrest Elizabeth and hang her as a spy. This warning shocked Elizabeth because she had no idea the rebels would hang a woman.

Because she could no longer send the ciphered messages by mail, Elizabeth set up an elaborate network to transport messages. The network went from the family's small farm just outside Richmond along five relay points to Colonel George Sharpe. Van Lew servants carried some of the messages in the soles of their shoes. Other agents hid messages in a hollowed-out egg placed among real eggs in a basket. A seamstress might carry a message hidden among her needles, threads, and scissors. Another might stitch the dispatch into her patterns.

Elizabeth often had to hide messages in her home

until an agent could carry them to Union officials. She used an ornamental iron fireplace in the library to conceal the papers. A small, crouched brass lion stood on each side of the grate. Elizabeth could raise the loose top on one of the lions like a box lid. She kept the secret documents in this shallow hole until messengers could transport them.

One time she needed to get some important information about Richmond's defenses to General Ulysses S. Grant. Elizabeth wrote her coded message, tore the message into narrow strips, and rolled each strip into a tiny ball. She grabbed a basket and hid all of the paper balls in it, but she had no messenger. Elizabeth headed for the market, where she hoped to find someone to carry the critical messages to the next relay station. As she walked along, a man whispered to her, "I'm going through tonight." Elizabeth pretended not to hear him because she feared a trap set by the secret police.

Her mind raced as she wandered around the market. The message had to get through. She wondered if she dared trust the man. He passed her again and repeated, "I'm going through tonight." Again Elizabeth hesitated. Something did not seem quite right. She returned home to find another way to have her message delivered. As she watched a group of Confederate soldiers march by her house the next day, she realized that the officer leading them was the man from the market.

Elizabeth used all of her energy to help protect Union soldiers. On the mansion's top floor under a sloping roof, she even had a secret room where she hid escaping prisoners. The room had a door that could be opened only by pressing a spring hidden behind an antique chest of drawers. A Union soldier hid in the room one time while Elizabeth's young niece visited her. That night when Elizabeth went upstairs to carry food to the soldier, the girl followed her aunt as far as the top of the staircase. She did not go any further because the dark shadows made the furniture look like ghosts. Frightened but curious, she paused on the last step. A thin man with a shaggy beard and long hair peered out of the room. He saw the niece who put her finger to her lips to warn him not to reveal her presence.

Later that night the niece overcame her fear, but not her curiosity. She went back upstairs by herself. She had watched her aunt open the door, and she pushed the hidden spring herself. The soldier again peered out and saw the young girl. He told her, "My, what a spanking you would have got if your aunt had turned around!" Her curiosity satisfied, the girl decided not to follow her aunt on any more trips to the top floor.

Only one of Elizabeth's coded messages has survived to present times. This message told of the Confederates' plan to move Federal prisoners from Richmond to Georgia. It warned the Union not to try to stop the move unless they had at least thirty thousand cavalry and another ten to fifteen thousand infantry. The message inspired a daring raid on Richmond led by twenty-one-year-old Colonel Ulric Dahlgren on February 28, 1864. Young Dahlgren had lost part of one leg in a battle prior to the raid. This handicap did not prevent his strong leadership in the raid that cost him his life. After he died, Confederate soldiers cut off one of his fingers to get a valuable ring and took his wooden leg and crutches to benefit their own soldiers. The rebels claimed they had found papers on Dahlgren stating he planned to burn and rob Richmond as well as kill Confederate President Jefferson Davis. When Richmond citizens heard this news, they rose up in anger. They demanded a "dog's burial, without coffin, winding sheet, or service" for Dahlgren.

Although Federal officials tried to keep his burial site secret, Elizabeth somehow discovered it. Her role in the recovery of his body has become one of her best-known feats. She organized a rescue party to dig up Dahlgren's body. Everyone knew the danger involved in the mission, but they found his body and put it in a metal coffin. They then loaded the coffin on a wagon and covered the coffin with tightly-packed, young peach trees. Elizabeth disguised herself in a cotton dress, buckskin leggings, and a huge calico sunbonnet. She rode on the wagon with the driver and led them through Richmond. They reburied the body in a safe place with a peach tree planted on the grave.

Elizabeth further vexed rebel officials when they came to her house to search for a horse. When the South continued to lose horses in battle, Confederate soldiers started taking animals from Richmond citizens. When soldiers heard that Elizabeth had a horse hidden at her home, they appeared at her door, determined to conduct a search. Elizabeth needed the horse for her spying activities. Someone had warned her about the search, and she had therefore planned for the soldiers' visit. She welcomed them and served them cake and tea. She then directed a servant to take them to the basement. The servant led the soldiers on a long, round-about way to the basement entrance, where she pretended to fumble for the right key. While the servant delayed the soldiers, Elizabeth brought the horse up another set of stairs to the library. She had prepared this room with a thick layer of straw to deaden the sound of the horse's hooves. The annoyed soldiers searched without success, while the horse feasted on the remains of their tea cake.

One of Elizabeth's most clever achievements involved her placement of an agent in Confederate President Jefferson Davis's house. The young woman, Mary Elizabeth Bowser, had once been a Van Lew slave. After the Van Lews freed their slaves, Elizabeth sent the girl north for an education.

When she returned to Richmond, Mary Elizabeth got a job as a maid in the Davis's house. Elizabeth then taught her to remember everything she heard at the dinner table. The young servant pretended to be dumb but listened intently to the conversations. She did a remarkable job of obtaining information as she served food. Elizabeth also taught Mary Elizabeth to save scraps from the Confederate president's wastebasket when she cleaned his study. The young maid, who used her photographic mind to remember every word of the messages she read on his desk while she dusted, became one of the Union's best agents.

From time to time the two women met at night near the Van Lew mansion. In order not to arouse suspicion, Elizabeth disguised herself as a country woman by wearing a bonnet, leggings, and a canvas coat. While driving a buggy around the grounds, she received Mary Elizabeth's reports. Jefferson Davis never did discover how information continued to leak from his house.

Elizabeth's spying often placed her in danger. She wrote in her diary that "from the commencement of the war until its close, my life was in continual jeopardy." Neighbors reported her activities, and detectives followed her so closely that she said, "I have turned to speak to a friend and found a detective at my elbow."

As Union troops once again marched toward Richmond, Elizabeth sent important information to General Ulysses S. Grant. He later told her over tea, "You have sent me the most valuable information received from Richmond during the war." With information such as that sent by Elizabeth, the Union won.

On April 2, 1865, Confederate General Robert E. Lee told President Davis to evacuate Richmond ahead of the Union troops' arrival. The rebels set fire to some tobacco warehouses before they ran away. Strong winds whipped the flames and caused them to spread to a powder magazine, which blew up and shattered windows all over town. Then an arsenal exploded, and people ran from the flying shells. Despite the danger, Elizabeth Van Lew and her servants climbed to the top of her mansion, where they displayed a nine-by-eighteen-foot United States flag with thirty-four stars.

Raising the Union flag angered Elizabeth's neighbors. They trampled her gardens and threatened to burn her house down. She faced them without fear. Elizabeth pointed her finger and called each one by name: "I know you, and you. General Grant will be in town in an hour. You do one thing to my home, and all of yours will be burned before noon!" The neighbors all left. As General Grant approached the burning city, he sent an aide to find Elizabeth and provide her with protection. The aide looked everywhere. He finally found her in the deserted Confederate Capitol, searching for documents to help the Union.

Soon after he became president, Ulysses Grant appointed Elizabeth as Richmond postmaster. The position paid her an annual salary of $4,000. After Grant left office she lost the job, but later took a clerk's position in the Washington post office department. After the party in power changed, she was demoted to the lowest clerk position with the smallest salary. Then a critical editorial appeared in several northern newspapers. The editor called Elizabeth a "troublesome relic." With her pride hurt, she resigned.

Elizabeth returned to Richmond when she could not get any other government position. There she led a lonely life with her niece and forty cats. Because she had supported the Union, her neighbors ignored her. She spent many hours alone in her garden. Her peculiarities became more apparent as she aged. The neighborhood children believed she was a witch. By the time Elizabeth's mother died in 1875, the family had few friends and could not even get enough pallbearers for her mother's funeral.

Elizabeth had not saved any money while working. Instead she had continued to help former slaves. She wrote: "I will tell you truly and solemnly that I have suffered for necessary food. I have not one cent in the world." The friends and family of a man she had cared for in Libby Prison came to her aid, providing her with an annual income for the rest of her life. They did this to recognize her service to Colonel Paul Joseph Revere, great grandson of the hero of the American Revolution.

Elizabeth became even lonelier after the death of her niece in 1889. Elizabeth wrote in her journal: "I live—and have lived for years—as entirely distinct from the citizens as if I were plague stricken . . . Rarely, very rarely, is our doorbell ever rung by any but a pauper, or those desiring my service." Almost penniless, Elizabeth Van Lew died on September 25, 1900, at the age of eighty-two. She would have agreed with and appreciated the epitaph engraved on her tombstone in Richmond's Shockhoc Hill Cemetery: "She risked everything that is dear to man—friends, fortune, comfort, health, life itself, all for one absorbing desire of her heart—that slavery might be abolished."

Although no picture exists of Belle Edmondson, one can imagine her resembling this Civil War-era woman dressed in the "Stars and Bars" of the Confederate Army.

Chapter Six

Belle Edmondson

Did the North finally get revenge on rebel spy Belle Edmondson? Did someone order the prescription that may have caused her death? No one knows because no newspaper reported her death, and no one issued a death certificate. After the Civil War ended, few people remembered her or her deeds.

Isabella Buchanan Edmondson was born in Pontotoc, Mississippi, on November 17, 1840, the eighth child of Andrew Jackson Edmondson and his second wife, Mary Ann Howard Edmondson. Nicknamed Belle, she grew into a warm-hearted and loving girl, but her wild ways made her mother describe her as the worst child ever. When she reached her teens, her parents tried to tame her by sending her to a local finishing school, where attempts to improve her behavior did not succeed.

When the Civil War began in 1861, the Edmondson family had just moved to Elm Ridge, a farm eight miles outside of Memphis, Tennessee. Belle's brothers, Jimmie and Eddie, immediately joined the Bluff City Grays and marched off to war. Her beloved mother died that same year. The loneliness brought on by these changes in her family may have led to Belle's association with Carlo Patti, a divorced concert violinist and composer. Young Belle found him worldly and interesting. At first she ignored his reputation for broken romances and horrified her family and friends by becoming engaged to him. However, their criticism and rumors about Patti's newest romance convinced Belle to end her relationship with him.

With the broken romance behind her, she began to look for another outlet for her energy. Because she hated the Yankees, she turned to spying, carrying mail, and smuggling. Both her love of the South and of danger attracted her to these activities in the Memphis area. In 1863, she started to work for Captain Thomas Henderson's Independent Scouts.

That same year she became engaged to a surgeon, Dr. Gratz Ashe Moses, but her new engagement did not stop Belle's work as a spy. In June she sent Captain Henderson a description of a man she suspected was a Yankee spy. Captain Henderson replied that they had just caught a man who fit her description, but they needed positive identification. He directed Belle to get someone to go to a court office for her and give a statement about the man. Henderson warned her not to try to make the report herself. He feared the enemy might hear about it and destroy her father's house or put her in prison.

Belle smuggled basic necessities across the Yankee picket lines, which were the dividing lines between Union-held and Confederate-held territories. Soldiers guarded these borders, allowing no one to cross over without a travel pass. A friend, Emily Barr, wrote that her family needed everything. They had lost all of their clothes except what they wore. They had no sheets, no pillow cases, no towels. Many families in the Confederacy were without food and other basic necessities. Belle asked permission to get some cotton to help her friends who needed clothes. Because the South could use the money they made from cotton to get weapons, Union General Ulysses S. Grant considered it contraband and did everything in his power to prevent Southerners from shipping cotton. Confederate officers denied Belle's request because "no one, not even the President . . . has a right to grant that authority."

Belle also carried hundreds of letters back and forth between rebel soldiers and their families. One night she worked until three o'clock in the morning to prepare four packages of 300 letters for the Confederate soldiers. To hide all of these illegal goods, Belle made use of the Southern styles of female clothing. Her hoop skirts hid letters, secret messages, medicines, and pistols. She used an elaborate hairdo to conceal messages and often hid letters and drugs among the mirror, powder, and perfume in her drawstring cloth purse. Belle once had eight yards of cloth, two hats, one pair of boots, one dozen buttons, two cords, eight tassels, and numerous letters under her clothes. She could not walk because of the weight, so she hired a ride across the picket lines. Belle made it through the lines with no problem, but she feared what would happen if guards stopped her.

Good news about the progress of the war encouraged Belle to continue her efforts, but then Dr. Moses left her. The reason for the unexpected end to their short engagement is uncertain. Dr. Moses may have heard the rumors about her earlier romance with Carlo Patti, or he may not have approved of the risks she took smuggling and gathering information. The doctor's action crushed Belle because she had truly loved him. For a while she considered suicide. One of Dr. Moses' friends wrote a letter to discourage her from such thoughts. He told her that someone who took daily risks to help others should protect herself. After the engagement ended, Belle continued to smuggle, carry mail, and spy in and around Memphis. Pickets sometimes searched her and she lost all that she carried. One week her diary entries showed her disappointment: "I did not smuggle a thing through the lines, except some letters."

Her diary also continued to show her sympathy for the rebel soldiers. In January 1864, she wrote: "Poor soldiers, this bitter cold weather I wish I had money to buy everything they need . . . God bless the Rebels. I would risk my life a dozen times a day to serve them— think what they suffer for us!"

The next day she went to Memphis, where she hoped to get a travel pass so that she could carry more letters to the soldiers. Lucie Harris, a friend, gave Belle her own pass, which she then used on February 27, 1864, to cross the picket lines. She wrote in her diary, "Tis a risk, yet we can accomplish nothing without great risk at times."

Although Belle continued her dangerous activities, she experienced both physical pain and loneliness. Separation from her brothers and sisters added to the loneliness that had begun with her mother's death. Chronic back pain forced her to stay in bed for days at a time. In her diary she wondered why she had so much sadness in her life: "For what am I living? Why is it that I am spared from day to day with no happiness myself?"

A surprise visit from her brother Eddie to the farm at Elm Ridge on April 6, 1864, cheered Belle. When he and his friends hid their horses in the woods away from the eyes of Yankee soldiers in a camp down the road, Belle and other family members took turns guarding the animals. Only a week later, the Yankee soldiers arrived at the farm. "A squad of 15 came and made us feed them and their horses—staid [sic] nearly three hours, hateful old thieves. I wish a squad of Confederates had come and captured the lot of them," she wrote in her diary.

Belle heard rumors that Union officials had issued a warrant for her arrest, although she did not know why. She went into Memphis on April 19 to try and get a travel permit and to collect letters to slip through the lines. She visited Captain Woodward, a Union official with whom she had become friendly, and asked him about the order for her arrest. He warned her to stay out of sight until he could learn more. The next day the captain brought her the bad news that Union officials did plan to arrest her on charges of carrying letters through the lines, smuggling goods, and aiding the rebels. Captain Woodward warned her to stay indoors because if she went outside, he would have to arrest her.

While in Memphis, Belle had hoped to attend the wedding of a friend, Jennie Eave. Instead she put on a heavy veil and went to a store to purchase things she would need if she had to leave home to avoid arrest. When she heard that some detectives were searching for her, Belle asked a friend to help her. The young woman went to see the provost marshal, the military head of police, to request a travel pass for herself and a friend, "Miss Edmunds." Belle used the pass to make it across the picket lines and back home.

Over the next few days she received several reports that many of her friends had to leave Tennessee. For her own safety Belle prepared to go south. She got her clothes ready, and friends smuggled across the line other things she would need. Her diary entry on May 18 shows her sadness about leaving home: "When, oh! when will this wickedness and strife end—my heart how sadly, and how sorely, it has been tried." Her father refused to let her black maid Laura go south with her. Belle felt all alone.

She moved from town to town as she made her way toward Mississippi over the next several months. Arriving there she went to Tupelo for the wedding of her younger sister Helen near the end of June, but the occasion was not a happy one for Belle. She felt the marriage would further separate her from her sister and add to her own loneliness. Her sister's failure to ask her to serve as her chief bridesmaid increased Belle's sadness. She reached Waverly outside Columbus, Mississippi, in July. Her worry grew when she heard discouraging news about the progress of the war. She also suffered a constant earache that caused partial deafness. Although her brother Eddie's monthly visits cheered her, she longed to see her maid Laura and her father. But she decided to return to Pontotoc, Mississippi, before she started the trip back home.

Pickets refused to let Belle and her companions board the Cold Water ferry unless they had a special pass. The next day she persuaded Confederate General James R. Chalmers to give her the pass. She went on without further trouble as far as Hernando, Tennessee, where she found a ten-year-old boy who agreed to drive her across the lines in a cart. Just two miles from Hernando, pickets refused to let them through. Noticing her trouble, an old man whispered to her to go back and get a saddle. Then he would help her run the pickets. She did so and successfully crossed the lines.

Although Belle received a warm welcome from Laura and her brother Eddie when she reached home that evening, her father ignored her. Because she loved him, she suffered from his neglect and lack of interest in her. She stayed at home only long enough to gather new supplies. She then left for her sister's house to start the journey south again. Loneliness was her constant companion. On November 17, 1864, Belle's twenty-fourth birthday, she wrote in her diary, "I wonder if anyone thought of me at home." The preserved part of her diary ends in November 1864.

Only a few details remain about the rest of her life. After the war she went back to Elm Ridge, where she continued to endure both loneliness and constant back pain. Occasional doses of morphine brought the only relief. Her sister Helen died in 1872, and her father died the following year. Brother Eddie, his wife and two children, moved to Elm Ridge, where they provided a home for Belle and another sister Joanna, who was also unmarried. Because many women of that time judged their value based on their relationship to the men in their lives, the single life was not a happy one.

Belle again became engaged in 1873 to a man identified only as Col. H, suspected by some as having once been a Yankee officer. Just two weeks after their surprise engagement announcement, Belle died at the age of thirty-three. The cause of her death remains uncertain. She may have died from smallpox, yellow fever, or cholera—the dreaded diseases of that time. She may have committed suicide or died from an incorrectly filled prescription.

In later years, Eddie's son spoke to interviewers. He told them the story he had heard about his aunt's death, which occurred before he was ever born. He said that Belle had died immediately after taking a prescription for a minor illness. Whoever filled the prescription at the Memphis pharmacy must have given her the wrong medication. After Belle took the first dose, she threw up her hands, yelled "Mother" once, and died. There is no way to verify her nephew's story. No one ever knew the real cause of her death or if her new fiancé had a part in it. Belle was buried beside her parents in the Elmwood Cemetery in Memphis. After her death, people soon forgot the daring deeds of the rebel spy Belle Edmondson. Only through her diary pages and her letters can one find any details of her life.

Belle Edmondson did not become as well known as other Confederate spies, such as Rose Greenhow or Belle Boyd. In fact she is often referred to as "the lost heroine of the Confederacy." Yet she contributed to the morale of Southern troops and their families. A letter to her from Major Thomas H. Price in 1863 shows the regard in which she was held: "God speed you in your angelic mission of imparting comfort and happiness to the soldiers of the South . . . with whom the name of Belle Edmondson will ever be a household word. You merit our gratitude; you have it, and I beg to assure you . . . your memory will ever be cherished."

Whether she accomplished as much or more than other Southern women who spied will never be known. Captain Thomas Henderson knew her service well. He showered her with praise and appreciation in his many letters to her. But Belle herself described her life as a pointless one in these sad lines from a poem she wrote in her diary: "Like a weary actor in a play, / Like a phantom in a dream, / Like a lost boat left to stray, / Rudderless in the stream—/ This is what my life has grown."

Sources

CHAPTER ONE: Sarah Emma Edmonds

p. 16, ". . . could carry a musket . . ." Pat Lammers and Amy Boyce, "A Female in the Ranks." *Civil War Times Illustrated* (January 1984): 26.

p. 16, ". . .the battle began to rage . . ." S. Emma E. Edmonds, *Nurse and Spy in the Union Army* (Hartford, Conn.: W.S. Williams & Co., 1865), 40.

p. 16, "Oh, how I want . . ." Lammers and Boyce, "A Female in the Ranks," 216-217.

p. 21, "He was a fated man . . ." Sylvia G. L. Dannett, *She Rode with the Generals* (New York: Thomas Nelson and Sons, 1960), 123.

p. 22, "Put this fellow . . ." Ibid., 124.

p. 22, "I was all alone . . ." Edmonds, *Nurse and Spy*, 119.

p. 26, "I assented, and joyfully . . ." Ibid., 170.

p. 27, "You will not have . . ." Ibid., 314.

p. 29, "EMMA E. SEELY[E] . . ." Richard Hall, *Patriots in Disguise: Women Warriors of the Civil War* (New York: Paragon House, 1993), 97.

p. 29, "No war ever developed . . ." Dannett, *Rode with the Generals*, 296.

CHAPTER TWO: Belle Boyd

p. 31, " Well, my horse is . . ." Louis A. Sigaud, *Belle Boyd: Confederate Spy* (Richmond, Va.: The Dietz Press, Incorporated, 1944), 1.

p. 32, "Men, every member . . ." Joseph Hergesheimer, *Swords and* Roses (New York: Alfred A. Knopf, 1929), 244.

p. 33, " I could stand it . . ." Ibid.

p. 33, " Whatever I heard . . ." Elizabeth D. Leonard, *All the Daring of the Soldier: Women of the Civil War Armies* (New York: W.W. Norton & Company, 1999), 27.

p. 35, " Here are two prisoners . . ." Ruth Scarborough, *Belle Boyd: Siren of the South* (Macon, Ga:. Mercer University Press, 1983), 29.

p. 35, " She pleads guilty . . ." John Bakeless, *Spies of the Confederacy* (Philadelphia: J.B. Lippincott Company, 1970), 153-54.

p. 39, " Miss Belle Boyd . . ." Hergesheimer, *Swords and Roses*, 252.

p. 40, "And so this is the . . ." Philip Van Doren Stern, *Secret Missions of the Civil War* (New York: Bonanzo Books, 1959), 104.

p. 41, "I hope that when I . . ." Ibid., 106.

p. 41, "My progress through . . ." John L. Papanek, ed., *Spies, Scouts, and Raiders: Irregular Operations* (Alexandria, Va.: Time-Life Editors, 1985), 48.

p. 45, "I feel like a criminal . . ." Richard F. Snow, "Belle Boyd." *American Heritage* 31 (Feb/Mar 1980): 95.

CHAPTER THREE: Pauline Cushman

p. 48, "Here's to Jeff Davis . . ." Agatha Young, *The Women and the Crisis: Women of the North in the Civil War* (New York: McDowell, Obolensky, 1959), 237.

p. 54, "Miss Cushman, I'm glad . . ." F.L Sarmiento, *Life of Pauline Cushman: The Celebrated Union Spy and Scout* (New York: John W. Lovell Company, 1890), 253.

p. 54, "She might be . . ." Harnett T. Kane, *Spies for the Blue and Gray* (Garden City, N.Y.: Hanover House, 1954), 188.

p. 55, "If found guilty . . ." Sarmiento, *Pauline Cushman*, 286.

p. 55, "General, come now! . . ." Ibid., 288.

p. 56, "That woman is . . ." Ibid., 297.

p. 59, ". . . among the women . . ." Leonard, *All the Daring,* 58.

CHAPTER FOUR: Rose O'Neal Greenhow

p. 62, "I am a Southern . . ." Kane, *Spies for the Blue*, 19.

p. 62, "You will know that . . ." Bakeless, *Spies of the Confederacy*, 10.

p. 63, "Tonight at whatever cost . . ." Ibid.

p. 63, "every capacity . . ." Kane, *Spies for the Blue,* 28.

p. 64, "McDowell [General Irwin] . . ." Papanek, *Spies, Scouts and Raiders*, 27.

p. 65, "Yours was received . . ." Bakeless, *Spies of the Confederacy,* 23.

p. 66, "Our President . . ." Papanek, *Spies, Scouts, and Raiders,* 27.

p. 69, "Watch from the corner . . ." Kane, *Spies for the Blue,* 46.

p. 70, "I have no power . . ." Alan Axelrod, *The War Between the Spies* (New York: The Atlantic Monthly Press, 1992), 62.

p. 70, "Mother's been arrested!" Papanek, *Spies, Scouts, and Raiders,* 29.

p. 72, "They . . . subjected me . . ." Rose Greenhow, *My Imprisonment and the First Year of Abolition Rule at Washington,* Electronic Edition (London: Richard Bentley Publisher, 1863), 95.

p. 72, "My castle has become . . ." Papanek, *Spies, Scouts, and Raiders,* 31.

p. 74, "But for you, there . . ." Leonard, *All the Daring,* 43.

p. 75, "Mrs. Rose O'N. Greenhow . . ." Kane, *Spies for the Blue,* 67.

CHAPTER FIVE: Elizabeth Van Lew

p. 78, "From the time I knew . . ." Kane, *Spies for the Blue,* 233.

p. 80, "Sad day. Three prisoners . . ." *Civil War Diaries,* available online from http://pixel.cs.vt.edu/aramsey/civil/vanlew/vanlewjuly1toaug121861.txt.

p. 82, ". . . there was not a moment . . ." Leonard, *All the Daring,* 55.

p. 84, "My, what a spanking . . ." William Gilmore Beymer, "Miss Van Lew." *Harper's Monthly Magazine* 123 (June 1911): 94.

p. 85, ". . . a dog's burial . . ." Kane, *Spies for the Blue,* 245.

p. 87, "from the commencement . . ." Beymer, "Miss Van Lew," 90.

p. 87, "I have turned to speak . . . " Ibid., 92.

p. 87, "You have sent me . . ." Ernest B. Furguson. *Ashes of Glory: Richmond at War* (New York: Alfred A. Knopf, 1996), 230.

p. 88, "I know you . . ." Kane, *Spies for the Blue,* 248-249.

p. 89, "I will tell you truly . . ." David D. Ryan, ed., *A Yankee Spy in Richmond: The Civil War Diary of "Crazy Bet" Van Lew* (Mechanicsburg, Pa.: Stackpole Books, 1996), 126.

p. 89, "I live—and have lived . . ." Beymer, "Miss Van Lew," 98.

p. 89, "She risked everything ..." Richard P. Weinert, "Federal Spies in Richmond," *Civil War Times Illustrated* 3, (February 1965): 34.

CHAPTER SIX: Belle Edmondson

p. 93, "... no one, not even ..." Loretta Galbraith and William Galbraith, eds., *A Lost Heroine of the Confederacy: The Diaries and Letters of Belle Edmondson* (Jackson: University Press of Mississippi, 1990), 63.

p. 94," I did not smuggle ..." Leonard, *All the Daring,* 75.

p. 94," Poor soldiers, this bitter ..." *Diary of Belle Edmondson,* January 2, 1864. Electronic Edition (Chapel Hill: University of North Carolina, 1998 online).

p. 95, "Tis a risk ..." *Diary of Belle Edmondson, February 27, 1864. Slaveholding South in the American Civil War* (Chapel Hill: The University of North Carolina Press, 1996), 238.

p. 95, "For what am I ..." Ibid.

p. 95, "A squad of 15 ..." Ibid., April 13, 1864.

p. 96, "When, oh! when will ..." Ibid., May 18, 1864.

p. 98, "I wonder if anyone ..." Ibid., November 17, 1864.

p. 99, "God speed you ..." Galbraith and Galbraith, *A Lost Heroine,* 36.

p. 99, "Like a weary actor ..." Ibid., 84.

Glossary

aide-de-camp: a military officer who acts as an assistant to a
superior officer
amnesty: a general pardon by a government for political
offenses
artillery: large-caliber firing weapons, such as cannons
auxiliary: a group that helps another group
bayonet: a knife which fits the muzzle end of a rifle and is used
in close fighting
blockade: the closing off of a city or harbor by hostile ships to
prevent trade and communication
briefing: the act of giving a short report, advice, or instructions
brigade: a military group composed of more than one unit
brogue: a strong Irish accent
cavalry: troops trained to fight on horseback
cipher: coded message
cleave: to stick to
Confederacy: the eleven Southern states that seceded from the
United States in 1860-61
contraband: goods banned by law from being imported or
exported

court martial: a military court set up to try persons
debut: the normal presenting of a girl to society
dispatch: an official written message usually sent with speed
embroidery: decoration of a fabric with needlework
ensign: a commissioned naval officer of the lowest rank
espionage: the act of using spies to obtain secret information
about another government
evacuate: to give up military possession of a town
Federal: having to do with the Union, or Northern states,
during the Civil War
fortitude: strength of mind that allows a person to endure great
pain or trouble
jeopardy: danger of risk or injury
justifiable homicide: killing of a person for a good reason
marksmanship: skill at shooting a gun or other weapon
malaria: a disease with chills, fever, and sweating; spread by
mosquito bites
memoirs: story about an author's personal experiences
morale: the state of the spirits of a person or group as shown by
their cheerfulness and willingness to do assigned work
morphine: a drug used to relieve pain; highly addictive
muslin: a plain, woven cotton fabric
needlepoint: decorative sewing done on a canvas
neutral: not favoring either side in a war or conflict
oath of allegiance: a formal pledge to support one's
government
ocher: an orange-yellow color
operative: a government agent
ovation: a show of public welcome and praise
parapet: an earthen or stone embankment to protect soldiers
from enemy fire
parole: the release of a prisoner on certain conditions before
his or her term has ended

picket: a soldier stationed to warn of an enemy's approach

propaganda: material distributed by people trying to convince others of their beliefs

provost marshal: a head of military police

rebel: a Confederate soldier during the Civil War

regiment: a military unit of ground troops

reinforcements: additional troops or equipment sent to support a military action

revolution: change in the government or social structure

riding habit: clothing worn by a horseback rider, especially prior to the twentieth century

royalties: shares paid to an author for sale of the author's work

rudder: a thin, flat piece of wood or metal used to direct a boat's course

sentry: a soldier posted at a given spot to prevent the entry of persons not wanted

smuggler: a person who illegally takes things in or out of an area

traitor: a person who betrays his or her country

Union: United States of America; the Northern states that did not secede during the Civil War

warrant: written permission for an officer to make a search, seizure, or arrest

winding sheet: a sheet for wrapping a dead body

Yankee: a Union soldier in the Civil War

Bibliography

Axelrod, Alan. *The War Between the Spies*. New York: The
    Atlantic Monthly Press, 1992.

Bakeless, John. *Spies of the Confederacy*. Philadelphia: J. B.
    Lippincott Company, 1970.

Beymer, William Gilmore. "Miss Van Lew." *Harper's
    Monthly Magazine* 123 (June 1911): 86-99.

Colman, Penny. *Spies! Women in the Civil War*. Cincinnati,
    Ohio: Betterway Books, 1992.

Dannett, Sylvia G. L. *She Rode with the Generals*. New York:
    Thomas Nelson and Sons, 1960.

Edmonds, S. Emma E. *Nurse and Spy in the Union Army*.
    Hartford, Conn.: W. S. Williams & Co., 1865.

Faust, Drew Gilpin. *Mothers of Invention: Women of the
    Slaveholding South in the American Civil War*. Chapel
    Hill: The University of North Carolina Press, 1996.

Furguson, Ernest B. *Ashes of Glory: Richmond at War*. New
    York: Alfred A. Knopf, 1996.

Galbraith, Loretta, and William Galbraith, eds. *A Lost Heroine
    of the Confederacy: The Diaries and Letters of Belle
    Edmondson*. Jackson: University Press of Mississippi,
    1990.

Greenhow, Rose. *My Imprisonment and the First Year of Abolition Rule at Washington* (Electronic Edition). London: Richard Bentley Publisher, 1863.

Hall, Richard. *Patriots in Disguise: Women Warriors of the Civil War.* New York: Paragon House, 1993.

Hergesheimer, Joseph. *Swords and Roses.* New York: Alfred A. Knopf, 1929.

Kane, Harnett T. *Spies for the Blue and Gray.* Garden City, N.Y.: Hanover House, 1954.

Lammers, Pat, and Amy Boyce. "A Female in the Ranks." *Civil War Times Illustrated* 22 (January 1984): 24-30.

Larson, Rebecca D. *Blue and Grey Roses of Intrigue.* Gettysburg: Pa.: Thomas Publications, 1993.

Leonard, Elizabeth D. *All the Daring of the Soldier: Women of the Civil War Armies.* New York: W.W. Norton & Company, 1999.

Papanek, John L., ed. *Spies, Scouts and Raiders: Irregular Operations.* Alexandria, Va.: Time-Life Editors, 1985.

Pinkerton, Allan. *The Spy of the Rebellion.* Lincoln: University of Nebraska Press, 1989.

Ross, Ishbel. *Rebel Rose: Life of Rose O'Neal Greenhow, Confederate Spy.* New York: Harper & Brothers Publishers, 1954.

Ryan, David D., ed. *A Yankee Spy in Richmond: The Civil War Diary of "Crazy Bet" Van Lew.* Mechanicsburg, Pa.: Stackpole Books, 1996.

Sarmiento, F. L. *Life of Pauline Cushman: The Celebrated Union Spy and Scout.* New York: John W. Lovell Company, 1890.

Scarborough, Ruth. *Belle Boyd: Siren of the South.* Macon, Ga.: Mercer University Press, 1983.

Sigaud, Louis A. *Belle Boyd: Confederate Spy.* Richmond, Va.: The Dietz Press, Incorporated, 1944.

Snow, Richard F. "Belle Boyd." *American Heritage* 31 (Feb/ Mar 1980): 94-95.

Stern, Philip Van Doren. *Secret Missions of the Civil War*. New York: Bonanzo Books, 1959.

Weinert, Richard P. "Federal Spies in Richmond." *Civil War Times Illustrated* 3 (February 1965): 28-37.

Young, Agatha. *The Women and the Crisis: Women of the North in the Civil War*. New York: McDowell, Obolensky, 1959.

Zeinert, Karen. *The Courageous Women of the Civil War*. Brooksfield, Conn.: The Millbrook Press, 1998.

WEBSITES

Civil War Web: Civil War Resource site
http://www.civilwarweb.com

Duke University Special Collections Library: Rose O'Neal Greenhow Papers
http://scriptorium.lib.duke.edu/greenhow/

University of Chapel Hill Libraries: Documenting the South, Diary of Belle Edmondson: Jan-Nov, 1864
http://docsouth.unc.edu/edmondson/menu.html

The Unknown Civil War: Civil War Resource site
http://www.unknowncivilwar.com/

Index

Henderson's Independent Scouts, 92, 99
childhood, 91-92
death, 98-99
engagements, 92, 94, 98

Forrest, Nathan Bedford, 54
Fort Sumter, 8, 10

Garfield, James A., 57
Granger, Robert S., 57
Grant, Ulysses S., 83, 87-88, 93
Greenhow, Rose O'Neal, *60*
childhood, 61-62
death, 75
marriage, 62
Greenhow, Robert, 62
Greyhound, 42

Hall, Allen, 24, 26
Hammond, John Swainston, 44-45
Hardinge, Samuel, 42, 44
Harris, Lucie, 94
High, Nathaniel Rue Jr., 45

Jackson, Stonewall, 39
Johnston, Joe, 65
Jordan, Thomas, 63

Lee, Robert E., 87
Libby Prison, *79*, 81, 89
Lincoln, Abraham, 10, 72

Mackell, Lillie, 70-71
McClellen, George B., 23, 29, 36
McNairy, Duval, 53
Morgan, John Hunt, 53
Morse, William, 15

New York Times, 59, 82
New York Tribune, 33, 35
Night Hawk, 75

Old Capitol Prison, 40-42, 44, 67, 72, 74

Pedden, S.E., 56-57
Pinkerton, Allan, 67-72, 82
Poe, Orlando M., 18

Schneider, Frederick, 29
The Seven Sisters, 48
Sharpe, George, 82
Shields, James, 36

Truesdail, William, 49-50

Van Lew, Elizabeth, *76*
childhood, 77-78
as "Crazy Bet," 81
death, 89
appointed postmaster, 88
Van Lew mansion, 77-78, *79*, 87

Wilson, Henry, 62-63
Wood, William, 40